VIOLENCE AGAINST WOMEN AND THE LAW

Mark A. Boyer and Shareen Hertel, Series Editors

International Studies Intensives (ISI) is a book series that springs from the desire to keep students engaged in the world around them. ISI books pack a lot of information into a small space—they are meant to offer an intensive introduction to subjects often left out of the curriculum. ISI books are relatively short, visually attractive, and affordably priced.

VIOLENCE AGAINST WOMEN AND THE LAW

DAVID L. RICHARDS AND JILLIENNE HAGLUND

PARADIGM PUBLISHERS
BOULDER | LONDON

Copyright © 2015 Paradigm Publishers

Published in the United States by Paradigm Publishers, 5589 Arapahoe Avenue, Boulder, CO 80303 USA.

Paradigm Publishers is the trade name of Birkenkamp & Company, LLC, Dean Birkenkamp, President and Publisher.

Library of Congress Cataloging-in-Publication Data

Richards, David L. (College teacher), author.
  Violence against women and the law / David L. Richards and Jillienne Haglund.
    pages cm. — (International studies intensives book series)
  Includes bibliographical references and index.
  ISBN 978-1-61205-148-2 (pbk : alk. paper) —
  ISBN 978-1-61205-757-6 (consumer ebook)
  1. Women—Crimes against.   I. Haglund, Jillienne, author.   II. Title.
  K5191.W65R53 2015
  345'.025082—dc23

                                                                2014033393

Printed and bound in the United States of America on acid-free paper that meets the standards of the American National Standard for Permanence of Paper for Printed Library Materials.

19 18 17 16 15   1 2 3 4 5

CONTENTS

ACKNOWLEDGMENTS

In the summer of 2008, we had an idea to create a unique dataset on violence against women. We created it and then spent the next six years repeatedly tearing it down and rebuilding it to get the data as correct as we could. People's interest in and/or consternation toward the stories our data told gave us the idea for this book. Along the journey, we benefited greatly from the support and criticism of a wide range of people. This is a better book for their counsel. We also worked with a number of research assistants who gave more to the project than we could possibly give back to them, and for their devotion and hard work we are eternally grateful. We'll certainly forget someone, but in the following paragraphs we try to thank as many as possible.

First, we want to thank Jennifer Knerr at Paradigm, and ISI series editors Mark Boyer and Shareen Hertel, for supporting us in writing the book we wanted to write, for their counsel on strengthening the final product, and for hanging in there with us during the final reconstruction of the dataset. We also wish to thank the anonymous manuscript reviewers for forcing us to provide a more clear statement of what we wanted to say.

Next, we give our sincere thanks to the many research assistants who helped us code, test, and recode our data. First, special thanks go to Celia Guillard and Stephen Petkis of the University of Connecticut (UConn), who went above and beyond in their assistance with the final data product. Also from UConn we wish to thank Kathleen Adams, Shaznene Hussain, David Schwegman, Jonathan Sykes, and Jack Zachary for all their hard work and dedication to getting things right. From Florida State University, we would like to thank Taylor Lee and Richard Farinas for their fantastic work on the project.

We wish to thank the organizers and participants at the conferences and workshops where we presented our data, methodology, and findings. We learned so much from our interactions with you. These forums included those sponsored by the American Political Science Association, the Department of Political Science at Emory University, the Economic and Social Rights Research Group at the Human Rights Institute at UConn, the International Human Rights Law Institute at DePaul University College of Law, the International Network on Quantitative Methods for Human Rights and Development, and the Protection Project at the Johns Hopkins University School of Advanced International Studies.

A special thanks to the kind folks at UN Women for taking the time to speak with us at length and in person about their work and their own data.

This book is also better off due to advice from K. Chad Clay, David Davis, Natalie Hudson, Manisha Desai, Amanda Kuppers, Kathy Libal, Mohamed Mattar, Heather Turcotte, and Richard Wilson.

Last, *but not at all least . . .*

David Richards wishes to thank his marvelous wife, Megan, for putting up with him throughout the writing process. David dedicates his portion of the book to his daughter Emily Elizabeth, with wishes that the world she meets is kinder than the one described in these pages. He owes great gratitude to Mandy Morrill, whose time as a domestic violence caseworker in southwest Missouri gave him an unvarnished view of domestic violence's means and costs, as well as a quick education in the limits of the law in providing protection and justice to victims of sexual violence. David also is indebted to the Human Rights Institute at the University of Connecticut for a faculty fellowship in 2012 that allowed him to complete a good deal of his contribution to the book. Finally, thanks to Roscoe, of course.

Jillienne Haglund wishes to thank all of her faculty advisors and mentors for their guidance and support as she pursued this research project while completing her dissertation and PhD. Their advice and feedback not only enabled this research to develop and improve, but also contributed to her growth as a scholar as this project evolved. She would also like to thank Justin, her parents (Lyndon and Kathy), and Chase and Kaitlyn, all of whom have provided incredible support, kindness, and patience throughout the completion of this project.

INTRODUCTION

The Problem

After a night out with her colleagues at Australian Broadcasting Corporation Radio, twenty-nine-year old Jill Meagher set off on the quarter-mile walk home to her Melbourne apartment. Colleagues offered to escort her back to the home she shared with her husband, but by all accounts Jill was confident enough both in the area and in herself to reach home safely alone. She was last seen that night at 1:30 am, her image captured through a storefront window by the camera of a security system. She was talking to her brother on her cell phone, trying to disengage from a strangely acting man in a blue hoodie. She was next seen six days later, her body having been found in a field. Forty-one-year-old Ernest Bayley was arrested before her body was found, and subsequently charged with rape and murder.

The public dialogue that ensued included a characterization of Ms. Meagher's ill fate as "random." For example, on September 29 the newspaper the *Australian* ran a headline reading "Community Shaken by Random Nature of Killing of Jill Meagher" (Gosper 2012), and several persons interviewed for that story made the same characterization. The use of the word "random" is interesting, as it implies something that couldn't be reasonably expected. Unexpected events can be scarier than those we can reasonably expect, as expectation brings the security of potentially being able to get ready for and control a situation; indeed, lack of control is scary. But was Jill Meagher's death really an isolated, unpredictable sexual assault and killing in a place and time where there exist structures that normally prevent such things from happening? Or could it have perhaps been avoided by better laws, better police enforcement of laws, and greater public empathy toward the issue of violence against women (VAW) in the place it occurred?

It is, of course, impossible to know what could have been in any particular case. We do know, however, that twenty-three-year old Stacey Scaife was threatened twice within six weeks by who she thought was the same man—two blocks from where Jill Meagher disappeared. We also know that she reported both incidents to police, who did not record her details of the incidents, made no follow-up inquiries, and did not ask her to file an official incident report (Carville 2012). Shortly after Jill Meagher's disappearance, media personality Catherine Deveny claimed that while riding her bicycle in July 2012 she was accosted by a man she thinks was Ms. Meagher's murderer (Deveny 2012). She did not report that episode until after Ms. Meagher's disappearance.

Indeed, much or most of the global pandemic of violence against women goes unreported. It is, in this sense, a stealth pandemic: its clandestine and stigmatic nature make it extra dangerous to both existing and potential victims. The Australian Bureau of Statistics reports that "more than 60 per cent of cases [of violence against women] go unreported" and "one in three Australian women is said to be a victim of domestic violence, including sexual abuse" (Lang 2012). The 2010 National Intimate Partner and Sexual Violence Survey in the United States found "nearly one in five women in the United States has been raped" (Black et al. 2011, 1). More than half of these rapes (51.1 percent) were reported as being committed by an intimate partner (ibid.). The 2000 National Violence Against Women Survey found that only "one-fifth of all rapes, one-quarter of all physical assaults, and one-half of all stalkings" by intimate partners were reported to police (Tjaden and Thoennes 2000). That is, underreporting rates were 80 percent, 75 percent, and 50 percent, respectively (ibid., v). In a statistical overview of domestic violence across India, Hackett (2011, 270) notes that underreporting in that country is, overall, "acute," with those crimes committed by husbands and relatives being "extremely underreported" (282).

The disappearance and death of Jill Meagher unleashed a storm of public grieving, anger, and frustration, much of it centered upon the belief that one of the reasons Ms. Meagher died is because Australian police do not take seriously reports by women who have been threatened. Were police there to have taken threats of violence against women more seriously, perhaps they might have apprehended Ms. Meagher's killer before his threats were brought to their deadly conclusion on an innocent female victim.

At a rally to protest rising rates of violence against women, held after Ms. Meagher's death, Penelope Swales, founder of Australia's Progressive Law Network, said that "changes are needed to how women victims of violence are dealt with by the law" and that when women complain, "they need to be taken seriously"

(Iaria 2010). The government of the Australian state of Victoria responded with a "pledge to force through tougher laws" (Ferguson 2012, 7). Unfortunately, rarely is any case an island and for some time Australia has been trying to leverage law to curb violence against women. After a review by the Australian Law Reform Commission finding the national definition of violence to be "too narrow" for its focus on physical conduct, an overhaul of Australia's Family Law Act went into effect in June 2012, enlarging the scope of "family violence" to include psychological as well as physical abuse (Pavey 2012, 33).

Calls to strengthen laws prohibiting and punishing violence against women are a common response to events increasing public awareness of the VAW pandemic. However, while still having faith in the law, we need to be careful in recognizing the limits of law's abilities, particularly in the short term. In Delhi, India, in December 2012, the brutal gang rape and resulting death of a twenty-three-year old woman named Jyoti Singh Pandey shook the country. Like the case in Australia, the crime resulted in calls for improvements to the way the legal code addressed the issue of violence against women. In India, subsequent changes included stricter penalties for rapists and the institution of more than seventy fast-track courts to adjudicate cases of sexual violence. But, as in the Australian case, willingness to enforce the law in India might reduce the impact of stronger laws. In June 2014, Ramsevak Paikra, the minister responsible for law enforcement in Chhattisgarh State, stated, "Such incidents [rapes] do not happen deliberately. These kind of incidents happen accidentally" (Agence France Press 2014).

Even given adequate enforcement, legal reforms themselves may be imperfect. In May 2014, one of the new fast-track Indian courts ruled that forced sex within marriage is not rape, as marital rape was not criminalized in the rush of legal reforms. Also, there may be persistent clashes between national and local-traditional legal structures. In January 2014, a village council in West Bengal sentenced a woman to gang rape for the crime of having planned to marry a man from outside her own village.

Toward a Greater Understanding of Violence against Women

This book is based on some seemingly simple questions, including these:

What differences in gender-violence laws exist across countries, and why?
What influences the adoption and content of gender-violence laws?
Where gender-violence laws have been adopted, how strong are the protections?

Are stronger legal prohibitions of and punishments for gender violence actually associated with improved well-being outcomes for women?

The way we approach answering these questions has roots in the cross-disciplinary research program investigating whether a state's having signed and/or ratified international human rights instruments has any effect on that state's actual human rights practices. There is some evidence that international law is associated with certain human rights protections (e.g., see Simmons 2009). While we stand on that foundational work, it is our strong belief that formal accession to international legal norms is *just the starting point* of the real story of the relationship between international law and the improvement of human dignity (via state respect for human rights law).[1] We expect that any effect international law may have on state human rights behavior comes via its effect on the creation and/or improvement of related domestic law. Further, all else being equal, we expect different outcomes from countries that differ in terms of the strength of their domestic gender-violence laws.

Most generally, we expect law—international and domestic—to work. Does this put too much of a burden of expectations upon law? We do not believe so, despite its aforementioned limitations. Simply because violence against women is widespread, despite many legal prohibitions and protections, does not mean laws that address it are unimportant or ineffective. All countries have both thieves and laws prohibiting theft. Yet no serious person would do away with these laws. And so it is with, say, rape laws. No rape law completely prevents rape, no matter how strongly it is written or enforced. However, what serious person would jettison legal prohibitions on rape simply because they are not perfectly effectual? Judging a legal framework on its lack of ability to eradicate crimes that date back to the earliest days of human history is unfair. On the other hand, we must leave room for the possibility that bad laws may be worse than no laws at all.

In Chapter 1 we offer an overview of the four types of violence against women discussed throughout the book: rape, marital rape, sexual harassment, and domestic violence. The conceptualizations of these forms of violence provided in this chapter help provide a common understanding among readers of the exact nature and scope of the forms of VAW. Taking time to define commonly understood terms such as *rape* may seem unnecessary at first, but as we point out in Chapter 4, what constitutes rape can have a great deal of latitude when we move beyond common understandings and toward the term's use for legal purposes. In addition, because later chapters introduce and use data based on these four VAW concepts, we have a duty to be transparent in what *we* mean when we use these terms.

Chapter 2 explores potential social, economic, political, cultural, and other factors that may bear on both the institution of VAW laws and the strength of these laws where they exist.

Chapter 3 investigates the relationship between international law and domestic law, and the ability of law to meaningfully address violence against women. This includes a section outlining feminist critiques of the law's ability to reduce violence against women. Chapters 2 and 3 both offer testable hypotheses, many of which are examined in the analyses later in the book.

Chapter 4 describes our creation of an original dataset of the strength of domestic laws addressing the four types of violence against women in 196 countries from 2007 to 2010. We created these data to improve upon existing data and to complement qualitative studies in order to fully understand the creation and effects of domestic gender-violence laws. Before the original data produced for this book, comparisons and analyses such as those herein were not possible.

Chapter 5 uses the dataset explained in Chapter 4 to test many of the hypotheses proposed in Chapters 2 and 3. The following are among the questions we attempt to answer via data analyses in Chapter 5:

Why do these laws exist in some places and not others?

Why are these laws stronger in some places than others?

Do these laws have any effect on outcomes?

Does international law drive the enactment of domestic VAW laws?

How is the presence/strength of these laws related to economic, political, and social institutions?

How does transnational society affect the presence/strength of domestic VAW laws?

Our empirical analyses produced many interesting findings. The broad significance of the findings presented in Chapter 5 is discussed in the book's conclusion. Unsurprisingly, we found that most countries have a good ways to go toward having an acceptable baseline of legal protections against VAW. There is interesting variation in what countries have what types of laws, however. Further, our analyses showed that women play an important role in efforts to create laws protecting them from gender violence. And law, where it exists, appears to affect societal outcomes in a way beneficial to women. Countries with stronger gender-violence laws generally have lower levels of gender inequality and higher levels of well-being than those without such laws, even controlling for a dozen possible explanations for these outcomes. Likewise, international law appears to have an effect: the greater the number of years a country has been a party to the Convention on the Elimination of All Forms of Discrimination against Women (CEDAW), the lower one can expect gender inequality and HIV rates to be and the greater one would expect legal protections against domestic violence to be.

Please note that we have also used maps in Chapter 5 of this book to help illustrate our findings. Color versions of those maps are available on this book's web page: http://www.paradigmpublishers.com/Books/BookDetail .aspx?productID=409755.

CHAPTER 1

FORMS OF VIOLENCE AGAINST WOMEN

In this chapter we provide a brief discussion of violence against women (VAW) as a human rights violation. We then explore the four forms of violence examined more closely in later chapters: sexual harassment, rape, domestic violence, and marital rape. In doing so, we briefly define each form of violence and discuss the causes, consequences, and prevalence of VAW globally.

Violence against women represents a global problem of pandemic proportions. Not only is VAW the leading cause of death among women between the ages of nineteen and forty-four, but it causes more deaths than malaria and car accidents combined, and gender-based violence contributes to as many deaths and disabilities for women as cancer (Johnson, Ollus, and Nevala 2008, 1). Given the prevalence of VAW, gender-based violence emerged onto the international human rights agenda in the 1990s. International women's rights activists and nongovernmental organizations (NGOs) increasingly mobilized to end gender-based violence following its omission from the primary women's rights treaty, the 1979 UN Convention on the Elimination of All Forms of Discrimination against Women (CEDAW) (Schuler 1992).

Pro-rights advocates gained momentum in the early 1990s. The 1993 UN World Conference on Human Rights in Vienna recognized women's rights as human rights, and included both public and private forms of violence (UN 1993).[1] The conference culminated in the adoption of the 1993 UN Declaration on the Elimination of Violence against Women (DEVAW) and the appointment of a special rapporteur to collect information on violence against women and make recommendations regarding its elimination (UN DEVAW 1993).[2] DEVAW defines violence against women as "any act of gender-based violence that results in, or is likely to result in, physical, sexual or psychological harm or suffering to women, including threats of such acts, coercion or arbitrary deprivation of liberty, whether occurring in public or in private life" (Article 1, DEVAW).

Violence against Women and Human Rights

Despite the drafting and adoption of DEVAW,[3] the inclusion of VAW on the human rights agenda has been relatively contentious. The difficult connection between violence against women and human rights stems from the view that human rights violations are those perpetrated by the state, not by private citizens. Governmental action and liberal principles apply to the public world, while individual autonomy governs the private sphere (Lacey 2004, 22). Therefore, when violence is committed by private individuals against women, individualism fails to challenge the public-private division and violence against women persists (Romany 1994). This state-centric approach to human rights perpetuates the view that the abuse of women is a cultural, private issue that is not political or public (Bunch 1990). Women have, historically and empirically, disproportionately engaged in the private sphere, leaving them outside the realm of political intervention (Lacey 2004). As a result, many forms of violence occurring in the home, such as domestic violence, marital rape, and numerous cultural practices, including forced marriages, dowry-related violence, and female genital mutilation, remain outside of the central political or legal issues of concern to state governments. However, VAW is deeply political, as "it results from structural relationships of power, domination, and privilege between men and women in society. Gender-based violence is central to maintaining those political relations at home, at work and in all public spheres" (Bunch 1990, 491). In other words, VAW reinforces, even perpetuates, structural discrimination against women in society.

Violence against women, then, represents a form of gender discrimination because it inhibits women from enjoying their rights and freedoms on a basis of equality with men (United Nations 1992, n. 3). The Universal Declaration of Human Rights (UDHR) provides for the protection of everyone "without distinction of any kind such as race, colour, sex, language . . . or other status" (Article 2). The primary principle of the international human rights regime entails recognition of the inherent dignity of all human beings, and therefore the equal and inalienable rights ascribed to all humanity (United Nations 1948). However, when society ascribes any one group (here, women) a "less-than-human" status, this becomes a human rights issue, as it prevents a group from enjoying its rights on an equal basis with other groups. The CEDAW committee reiterates this sentiment in stating that violence against women is "directed against a woman because she is a woman" or is violence that affects women disproportionately, meaning that men and women are not at the same risk for experiencing these types of violence (True 2012).[4] Further, VAW disproportionately affects women *everywhere*. In reflecting on the women's rights movement in the 1980s, Bunch (2012, 31) claims, "the similarity in problems, social attitudes, and feminist strategies was striking—even while the manifestations of violence varied as they intersected with the particulars of culture, race, class or other factors."

Further, the link between VAW and experiences of torture highlights the political and public nature of this type of violence. In the 1980s, feminists began to draw comparisons between the sexual torture of Latin American female political prisoners during the dirty wars in Latin America and VAW. They recognized the similarity between their experiences of abuse at home and the violence experienced by political prisoners in jails (Copelon 1994 and 2003). These experiences highlighted the exclusion of women's rights from the human rights agenda. The notion of rape and battery, among other forms of VAW, as torture largely gained momentum through the activities of Amnesty International and contributed to the placement of VAW on the international human rights agenda (Amnesty International 2001).

From a human rights framework, when states fail to uphold their responsibilities to citizens by not protecting women from violence, the state has committed a human rights violation (Merry 2006; Thomas and Beasely 1993; Bunch 1990). Failing to prosecute murder, assault, or harassment against women in the home with the same stringency or severity as when those forms of violence occur under other circumstances indicates that state agents are participating in discrimination on the basis of gender (Merry 2006, 22). This is because neither international human rights law nor state law can be neutral when it does not provide meaningful recourse for women; it empowers the perpetrator of abuse (Romany 1994).

Despite the momentum gained by examining VAW from a human rights framework, its inclusion in the international human rights agenda was not without opposition. Opponents of the idea referenced the UDHR as designating human rights violations to be only those perpetrated by states against citizens. However, as Susan Okin (1981, 239) notes, "The Declaration by no means [has as] its sole intent to warn governments against their own potential for violation. To the contrary, besides hardly mentioning governments at all, it suggests strongly that at least some of the obligations correlative to the rights it pronounces fall on individuals as well as on states." Violence occurring in the private context of intimate partner relationships or in the home does not remove the state's responsibility for holding non-state private perpetrators of violence to account for their violations of the human rights of others (Reilly 2009).

A recent European Court of Human Rights case provides an example of the controversy surrounding state intervention in violent intimate-partner relationships. For years, Nahide Opuz and her mother requested police protection from domestic abuse perpetrated by Nahide's husband. In 2002 he murdered Nahide's mother. In 2009 the court found Turkey responsible for failing to take reasonable measures to prevent domestic violence and to protect Nahide's mother's right to life; it found Turkey in violation of the right not to be subject to torture or cruel, inhuman, or degrading treatment.[5] This landmark decision by an international court provides an indication of the extent of state responsibility under international law with respect to VAW. More specifically, the decision emphasizes that "domestic violence is not a private or family matter, but an issue of public interest that demands effective state action" (van Gulik 2012, 226).[6]

In opposition to the role of the state in VAW, some feminist scholars highlight the problem of women seeking protection from the state, arguing that "the heavy price of institutionalized protection is always a measure of dependence and agreement to abide by the protector's rules" and that surrendering the codification of legal protections to a state dominated by masculine powers is particularly dangerous (Brown 1995, 169). Using the state as a solution is problematic because "to be 'protected' by the same power whose violation one fears perpetuates the very modality of dependence and powerlessness marking much of women's experience" (Brown 1995, 169–170).

However, despite these arguments, the international human rights regime utilizes international legalization as one of the most important tools to secure the protection of rights (Simmons 2009). Because international law is largely self-enforcing, "a government that does not adopt, fund and implement all necessary laws and actions to prevent and to punish violence violates international human rights law" (van Gulik 2012, 223). Even Brown (1995, 169) concedes that "minimal levels of protection may be an essential prerequisite to freedom." VAW represents a widespread and prominent human rights violation, and as such, the state faces a responsibility to protect women from violence.

What Is Violence against Women?

Women face violence both in the context of the home (perpetrated by family or an intimate partner) and outside the home (perpetrated by various individuals, including government agents, employers, coworkers, and teachers). In what follows, we provide a brief survey of four forms of VAW occurring in the public and private spheres: sexual harassment, rape, domestic violence, and marital rape. The extent to which each form of violence occurs in the public or private sphere varies, with sexual harassment occurring largely in the public sphere, and rape, domestic violence, and marital rape representing increasingly private forms of violence. In what follows, we define each form of VAW and provide an overview of the causes, consequences, and prevalence of each type. In later chapters, we examine legal protections related to these four forms of violence.

SEXUAL HARASSMENT

Defined. Sexual harassment represents a form of gender-based violence occurring largely in the public sphere. The United Nations Entity for Gender Equality and the Empowerment of Women (2008) defines sexual harassment as

> any unwelcome sexual advance, request for sexual favor, verbal or physical conduct or gesture of a sexual nature, or any other behavior of a sexual nature that might reasonably be expected or be perceived to cause offense or humiliation to the female victim by a non-partner. If such conduct interferes with work, it is made a condition of employment and may create an intimidating, hostile, or offensive work environment. Sexual harassment may include a pattern of behavior or a single incident.

Despite the variation in legal definitions of sexual harassment around the world, experts have developed a general consensus regarding actions that constitute sexual harassment. Sexual harassment includes actions related to sex or sexual conduct, the conduct is unwelcome and usually not mutually desirable, and the conduct affects the terms or conditions of employment (Webb 1994). Sexual harassment can take two forms: *quid pro quo harassment* involves job benefits or an exchange such as a pay raise, promotion, or continued employment conditioned on the victim engaging in sexual behavior, while *hostile-working-environment harassment* involves conduct of a sexual nature that creates an uncomfortable environment, including intimidating or humiliating working conditions for women (ILO 1996). Sexual harassment involves a variety of forms of behavior, and can include physical, verbal, or nonverbal conduct (McCann 2005). The key to defining sexual harassment is the inclusion of the "unwelcomeness standard," which is intended to draw a distinction between "inoffensive and unacceptable behavior according to the context in which it takes place" (McCann 2005, 3).

Causes. Sexual harassment is often rooted in two types of relationships of unequal power. MacKinnon (1979, 1) claims, "The major dynamic is best expressed as the reciprocal enforcement of two inequalities. When one is sexual, the other material, the cumulative sanction is particularly potent." First, like most other forms of violence against women, sexual harassment is the result of the use of male sexuality to reinforce male power, often rooted in patriarchal social structures in society (MacKinnon 1979; Wise and Stanley 1987). As such, sexual harassment constitutes a form of violence against women "directly and clearly related to hegemonic masculinity and subsequently taps more potently into structural and culturally sanctioned roles and meanings (masculine-feminine, male-female, heterosexual-homosexual) that are core components of social stratification" (Morgan and Gruber 2011, 87). That is, sexual harassment is thought to be deeply rooted in both the use of sexual behavior and the abuse of power (MacKinnon 1979).

The second inequality occurs in the context of employment or other situations in which hierarchical relationships exist, including unwanted advances between employer and employee or between teacher and student. Of course, sexual harassment also includes advances by coworkers, subordinates, fellow students, or other persons, regardless of hierarchical relationship. However, research shows that those most at risk of sexual harassment are individuals working in environments overpopulated by men (Morgan and Gruber 2008; Willness et al. 2007). Further, the risk of sexual harassment is higher when the necessity of conforming to masculine norms determines an individual's work performance (i.e., women working as police officers, firefighters, miners, and the like) (Gruber and Morgan 2005). Work requiring interactions with men in intimate settings creates a higher risk for sexual harassment as well. For example, nurses experience harassment relatively more often than those working in more bureaucratic or professional venues (Hesketh et al. 2003; Kane-Urrabazo 2007).

Consequences. Sexual harassment exhibits numerous adverse effects on women's mental and physical health. One study found a strong association between military-reservist victims of sexual harassment and many medical conditions, including depression, eating disorders, and other mental illnesses (ILO 1996; Street et. al 2008). Further, sexual harassment victims often lose trust not only in the perpetrator of abuse, but also in the leadership of the organization where the harassment occurs, and victims may decline career opportunities or leave their place of employment as a result (ILO 1996; Murray, Sivasubramaniam, and Jacques 2001).

Employers also face costs when sexual harassment occurs in the workplace, including the loss of productivity and an inability to hire individuals who may fear further sexual harassment (ILO 1996). For example, in one Canadian survey, nearly one-third of victims of sexual harassment reported that their jobs had been affected (Crocker and Kalembra 1999).

Finally, societal costs are large, including long-term reintegration of victims, legal expenses, and unemployment welfare benefits (ILO 1996). One study on sexual harassment in the US Armed Forces found costs associated with recruiting, training, transfers, grievances, counseling, and administration as a result of sexual harassment totaled $250 million (1994 dollars) for the Army as a whole (Faley et al. 1999).

Prevalence. Sexual harassment represents a widespread and prevalent form of violence against women. It occurs across all societies around the world, regardless of socioeconomic status or education. Sexual harassment typically occurs in the workplace and in schools (Morgan and Gruber 2011). Survey research assessing the prevalence of sexual harassment shows the problem to be pervasive. In fact, one survey of all US government employees found 44 percent of all female government employees had experienced some form of sexual harassment within two years of the survey (United States Merit Systems Protection Board 1994). Other studies find that 26 percent of female Japanese civil servants experienced sexual harassment (Huen 2007), and a Canadian survey showed that 50 percent of female respondents had experienced sexual harassment within two years of the survey (Canadian Human Rights Commission 1983). In a recent survey, the Australian National Human Rights Commission found that approximately one in four women (25 percent) had been sexually harassed in the workplace in the previous five years and one-third of women had been sexually harassed in their lifetimes (Broderick 2012).

RAPE

Defined. Legal definitions of rape have changed over time and differ substantially across and even within states. Many laws define rape as "an act of penile/vaginal penetration committed by some degree of force or the threat of force" (Berger, Searles, and Neuman 1988; Estrich 1987). Most early definitions were based on three elements: penetration, the use of force, and the absence of consent (Spohn and Horney 1992). However, the growth of the feminist movement in the 1970s contributed to a redefinition of rape, as feminists considered laws to be incomplete in identifying the specific acts that constitute rape, the tactics perpetrators use to commit such acts, and degrees of coercion and consent involved in these acts (Fischer 1989; McMahon 2011). Research in the 1980s indicated that women reported many forced or coerced sexual acts in addition to the standard definition of rape (Gavey 2005). With respect to coercion, feminists emphasized the importance of rape as an issue of power and control and shifted the focus from rape perpetrated by strangers to rape perpetrated by acquaintances (Brownmiller 1975; Griffin 1971; Koss, Gidycz, and Wisniewski 1987; Russell 1975).

Causes. Rape represents a crime of power (Brownmiller 1975). The extent of power and control differs depending on the societal context in which rape takes place. Specifically, women's experiences differ based on the context within which the acts of sexual violence are committed (Gavey 2005; MacKinnon 2006). Societies in which male control and power remain deeply entrenched in culture make it difficult to understand coercion and consent in the same way as it might be understood in other societies. As a result, women may never consent, as coerced psychological control is always present in a culture in which male dominance and control are the norm. Campbell and Townsend (2011, 99) claim, "It is likely that women do experience multiple instances of sexual coercion in their sexual lives, and there is no common nomenclature to express these events and their meaning."

Further, legal problems inhibit the ability of law enforcement to hold perpetrators accountable and, absent effective recourse, rape persists in many societies. For example, legal experts may find strict legal definitions based on coercion difficult to apply in practice given that "there is a continuum of degrees of coercion. On one end is physically forced compelling and on the other end are fully consensual acts. Between these two ends are many shades of gray" (Hamby and Koss 2003, 252). Court cases involving accusations of rape often hinge on whether the victim consented. However, it is difficult for these cases to hold up in court, as rape does not typically permit the discovery of corroborating evidence, such as additional witnesses or visible physical harm or injury (McLean and Goodman-Delahunty 2008). As a result of these legal-definitional difficulties, the past two decades have witnessed US states replacing the term *rape* with *sexual assault* or *sexual violence,* both of which include acts up to and including rape. The Centers for Disease Control and Prevention (CDC 2009) identifies "a range of offenses, including a completed nonconsensual sex act (i.e., rape), an attempted nonconsensual sex act, abusive sexual contact (i.e., unwanted touching), and non-contact sexual abuse (e.g., threatened sexual violence)" under the category of sexual violence. However, the failure to specifically name the crime of rape (or domestic violence, and the like) may prove difficult in terms of punishing the perpetrators in court of law.

In addition to legal inconsistency as a causal factor in the prevalence of rape, armed conflict often exacerbates violence against women, including "random acts of sexual assault by both enemy and friendly forces, or mass rape as a deliberate strategy of genocide," as well as military sexual slavery, forced prostitution, forced pregnancies, and gang rape (WHO 1997a). The changing nature of warfare provides one explanation for the increase in the use of violence against women during armed conflict (Ward and Marsh 2006). Civil wars and regional conflicts, often among different ethnic, religious, or racial groups, are on the rise, largely replacing interstate conflicts. The shift from interstate to intrastate and regional conflict triggers an increased focus on civilians as targets during conflict, and while men represent a greater proportion of casualty totals, "women and children are disproportionately targets and constitute the majority of all victims of contemporary armed conflicts" (UNSC 2002).

Increased VAW during conflict led to the passage of UN Security Council Resolution 1820 in 2008, which addressed the issue of sexual violence during times of conflict and called for "the immediate and complete cessation by all parties to armed conflict of all acts of sexual violence against civilians with immediate effect." Violence against the female population represents a weapon of war, a tool used to achieve military objectives such as ethnic cleansing, spreading political terror, breaking the resistance of a community, rewarding soldiers, intimidation, or to extract information" (Amnesty International 2009; Medicins Sans Frontieres/Doctors without Borders 2009). Soldiers use systematic sexual violence to destabilize populations and destroy community bonds publicly to bring about shame and humiliation (Ward and Marsh 2006). Such was the case in East Timor, where members of the Indonesian military raped women in front of their families.

Violence against women as a tool for ethnic cleansing in conflict may include public rape used to initiate flight or expulsion of entire communities, as well as "forced impregnation, mutilation of genitals and intentional HIV transmission" (Ward and Marsh 2006, 4). During the Bosnian conflict, Serbian political and military leaders used rape as a tool to carry out a policy of ethnic cleansing, with two specific objectives: to "create more Serbs to further the Serbian nationalist ideology, and to create more soldiers to defend the country" (Salzman 2006). Serbs often held Bosnian Muslim women captive until late in their pregnancy to prevent abortion (Ward and Marsh 2006).

Consequences. Rape, as a form of VAW, results in various physical- and mental-health consequences for individual women and society as a whole. One study found that 50–90 percent of rape survivors have genital injuries (Sommers 2007). Violence against women also influences women's mental health, leading to problems of depression, anxiety, substance abuse, and suicidal behaviors (Bonomi et. al 2006; Carbone-Lopez, Kruttschnitt, and Macmillan 2006; Coker et al. 2002). Further, rape may lead to unwanted or early pregnancy. Early pregnancy, particularly during early or middle adolescence, is associated with negative health outcomes for both women and children. Unwanted pregnancies often result in many women choosing abortion. However, abortion remains illegal or prohibitively expensive for women in many countries, which potentially leads to an increase in illegal abortion and adverse health problems (WHO 1997b). One study in India found that 20 percent of all pregnancies of adolescent abortion seekers occurred because of forced sex (Divekar, Natarajan, and Purandare 1979). Further, in many countries rape leads to sexually transmitted diseases, including HIV/AIDS. Studies also link rape to psychological damage and mental-health problems. Blumel et al. (1993) estimated the costs of domestic violence, rape, and sexual assault in Australia, finding the personal costs—including legal accommodation, courts, emergency services, police, health counseling, referral, and lost earnings—to amount to A$620 million. Miller, Cohen, and Wiersma (1996) find the cost of violence, including rape, as a result of property damage and loss, medical care for injuries, insurance, victim services, lost earnings, and lost work to be US$105 billion and both the direct and indirect costs of rape to be US$7.5 billion.

The costs of conflict-related violence are high, as society must absorb not only costs associated with post-conflict building and reconstruction, but the physical and psychological health effects of VAW. The need to reintegrate women in society means an additional cost in post-conflict settings. Women not only need medical treatment, protection, legal justice, and psycho-social care, but social and economic services to assist in reintegration and allow them to provide for their families (True 2012).

Further, with the passage of UN Security Council Resolutions 1820 and 1889, addressing sexual violence in conflict, international attention shifted to prosecution and punishment of perpetrators of gender-based violence during conflict. The international community improved funding to provide medical and judicial support to sexual-violence conflict survivors and "significant international resources have been made available to prosecute perpetrators of sexual violence by bolstering legal institutions and judicial capacity and establishing legal aid and remedies for primarily women victims" (True 2012, 129). The costs of gender-based violence during conflict remain high and place a large financial burden on communities devastated by conflict as well as the larger international community.

Prevalence. The CDC's National Intimate Partner and Sexual Violence Survey found that nearly one in five women (18.3 percent) in the United States have been raped (Black et al. 2011). Further, 35 percent of women worldwide have experienced physical and/or sexual intimate-partner violence or nonpartner sexual violence (Garcia-Moreno and Pallitto 2013).

The crime of rape is pervasive and determining its prevalence proves difficult, as rape is vastly underreported. Empirical evidence shows that any concern of false accusations does not compare to the number of rapes that are never reported or to the number of rapists never prosecuted or convicted in a court of law. Scholars and policymakers estimate that between 75 and 95 percent of rapes are never reported to the police (HMIC 2007).[7] Women have numerous reasons for failing to report rape, but a primary reason involves perceptions of what constitutes rape; that is, many view rape as perpetrated by strangers and involving physical injury (HMIC 2007, 8). Other reasons often cited for not reporting include "personal and societal barriers, lack of trust in or fear of secondary victimization by the criminal justice system, and sometimes logistical barriers . . . the nature and severity of the assaults and the support structures available to victims" (Johnson, Ollus, and Nevala 2008, 152). Of the small number of rapes reported to police or other law-enforcement officials, only 37 percent are prosecuted (Tjaden and Thoennes 2006).

While rape represents a particularly prevalent form of VAW in society, rape and sexual violence are exacerbated during violent conflict or crisis (WHO 1997a). As discussed previously, rape is one of the most common forms of gender-based violence perpetrated during conflict. Soldiers relied on rape as a tool of war in Bosnia and Herzegovina, Burma, Burundi, Colombia, the Democratic Republic of the Congo, Liberia, Serbia, Sierra Leone, Somalia, and Sudan, among numerous other conflicts (Fontes and McCloskey 2011). Some estimates suggest that 20,000 to 50,000 women were raped during the 1992–1995 conflict in Bosnia and Herzegovina, and the United Nations reports that an estimated 250,000 to 500,000 women and girls were raped in the course of the Rwandan genocide (UN 1996; Ward 2002). For example, in a sample of Rwandan women surveyed in 1999 by the Rwandan NGO Association of Widows of the Genocide (Avega), 39 percent of women reported being raped during the 1994 genocide, while 72 percent reported knowing someone who had been raped (Ward 2002, 27). One Rwandan genocide rape survivor, Perpetue, recalls that "for two days, [she] and eight other young women were held and raped . . . one after another" (Nowrojee 1996, 43). Perpetue was also subjected to vaginal mutilation at the hands of militia groups, leaving her with long-lasting injuries.

Women remain at heightened risk for violence at all stages of conflict, including in post-conflict situations. Female refugees face a high risk of sexual violence upon flight from conflict-ridden environments. Many women are forced to flee without the safety of male relatives or other community members and "without money or other resources, displaced women and girls may be compelled to submit to sex in return for safe passage, food, shelter, or other resources" (Ward and Marsh 2006, 7). Further, women in internally displaced persons camps have few protections from sexual violence; women who must leave camps in search of resources, such as firewood or water, often fall victim (Ward and Marsh 2006).

Also, in many cases, women face an increased risk of violence during post-conflict reconstruction because programs do not always specifically address the needs of women or the "long-standing patriarchal traditions that discriminate against women" (Ward and Marsh 2006, 9). For example, inheritance laws in Rwanda prohibited women from possessing the property of deceased male relatives unless named specifically as beneficiaries. This left many women without resources, including homes, and many impoverished women were drawn into the sex trade (Amnesty International 2004). Further, victims of rape may be ostracized by their families or communities as a result of sexual violence experienced during conflict (ibid.).

DOMESTIC VIOLENCE

Defined. Domestic violence includes actual or threatened physical or sexual violence, or psychological abuse by a spouse, ex-spouse, current or former boyfriend, intimate partner, or child and includes violence committed by cohabiting or noncohabiting partners (Basile and Black 2011; Saltzman et al. 1999). This may include physical abuse that causes injury, including but not limited to hitting, kicking, slapping, grabbing, punching, choking, burning, beating, pushing/shoving, and throwing dangerous objects. Sexual abuse may include sexual coercion, rape, and sexual assault, among other forms of violence. Psychological abuse includes threatening violence; shouting and yelling; use of degrading, insulting, or humiliating language; ostracism; stalking; or intentional destruction of property (Basile and Black 2011).[8] Scholars now differentiate between *verbal* psychological aggression, which includes yelling, humiliating, and demeaning an intimate partner, among other acts of violence, and *instrumental* psychological aggression, which includes coercive and controlling behaviors (Basile and Black 2011; O'Leary 1999). These types of domestic abuse do not represent mutually exclusive categories, as physical abuse is often combined with psychological, financial, or other forms of abuse, such as isolation (Schneider et al. 2008).

Causes. Scholars across multiple disciplines highlight numerous potential causal factors to explain the occurrence of domestic violence. The World Health Organization, among other international and domestic actors, applies an ecological model to understand intimate-partner violence (Dahlberg and Krug 2002). The ecological model focuses on the role of multiple levels of influence in the behavior of individual perpetrators (Chalk and King 1998; Heise 1998).

The first level emphasizes psychological approaches and individual-level factors, including personal attributes and gender socialization (Jordan 2009). At this level, individual characteristics (educational attainment, substance abuse, and the like) influence the likelihood of being a victim or perpetrator of violence. The second level explores the role of the family and relationships within the family. For example, economic control within the family, specifically male control of wealth and decision making in the home, often plays a crucial role in the occurrence of intimate-partner violence. In families where women work as part of the informal economy (engage in unpaid work in the family or in the private sphere), the bargaining power in the family may tip toward the male employed in the formal economy (True 2012, 30). This gendered division of power lends itself to relationships in which women become trapped in violent situations at home or work and the perpetuation of violence is used as a tool to control or subordinate an intimate partner. The third level of the ecological model focuses on the community, including schools, workplaces, and neighborhoods (Dahlberg and Krug 2002). For example, characteristics such as residential mobility, diversity, population density, and unemployment are often associated with the probability of being a victim or perpetrator of gender-based violence.

Finally, the fourth level of the ecological model includes societal factors such as health, education, and economic and social policies that create high levels of economic or social inequality (Dahlberg and Krug 2002). For example, globalization encourages the growth of participation of women in the labor force or creates an environment in which more women join the formal economy, often in low-paying, insecure jobs. As a result of the entry of women into the formal economy, many men face a loss of employment and choose to reassert their power over women through violence (True 2012, 31). The causes of domestic violence discussed here by no means constitute an exhaustive list. Various factors often coexist and mutually reinforce one another, contributing to the prevalence of intimate-partner violence. Given the multifaceted nature of domestic violence, and VAW generally, there are multiple levels on which to confront this problem. In later chapters, we will explore and examine various societal (state)-level factors empirically.

Consequences. Victims of domestic violence face various physical and mental health problems, similar to those associated with rape and intimate-partner violence. The physical and psychological effects of VAW on individual victims also place a financial burden on society, both directly and indirectly. Direct costs may include added healthcare costs, such as medical treatment for short- and long-term physical and mental health problems. Of course, the level of healthcare costs depends on the extent to which health care is publicly or privately funded, and these costs are distributed differently across individuals and the public cross-nationally. One study by the National Center for Injury Prevention and Control (2003) estimated costs incurred from injuries and deaths, including medical and mental health care as well as lost productivity and lost lifetime earnings for VAW victims killed in the United States. The study estimated an annual cost of $5.8 billion in 1995. Intimate-partner violence often exhibits intergenerational patterns; numerous studies find links between childhood physical and sexual abuse, as well as witnessing violence between other family members, and the likelihood of perpetrating abuse (Fang and Corso 2008; Gil-González et al. 2007; Riggs, Caulfield, and Street 2000). In other words, violence experienced during childhood represents a high risk factor for perpetrating violence. The generational perpetuation of violence against women indicates that this public-health problem is likely to continue along family lines, increasing the costs for individuals and society. Violence against women also often influences the victims' sexual and reproductive health and may result in unwanted and early pregnancy and heightened risk of contracting HIV/AIDS and other sexually transmitted diseases (WHO 1997b). Intimate-partner violence also plays an adverse role in the mental health of women, resulting in mental illnesses and disorders such as depression, anxiety, substance abuse, and suicidal behaviors, among others (Bonomi et. al 2006; Cabone-Lopez, Kruttschnitt, and Macmillan 2006; Coker et al. 2002). One study reports that abused women in Nicaragua are six times more likely to experience mental health issues than non-abused women (Stark and Flitcraft 1991).

Society also bears direct costs related to justice, including the costs of investigation and prosecution of perpetrators, as well as penal costs, such as victim compensation, administration of community sentences, and court trials (Day, McKenna, and Bowlus 2005; WHO 1997b). Social costs may include those associated with the provision of public services and funding for women's shelters, support groups for victims of violence, and social welfare services for abused women (Day, McKenna, and Bowlus 2005; Morrison and Orlando 1999; WHO 1997b). Other social costs involve education, such as the need for special education for child witnesses of violence, or school programs designed to reduce violence against women (Day, McKenna, and Bowlus 2005)

The financial burden placed on society also includes indirect costs such as the loss of productivity in both the formal and informal employment sectors. Such economic costs stem from factors including women's "lost time at work and reduced attention, the time her co-workers spend covering for her, the time she may spend in the restroom or on the phone with friends or family, actual time she may need to take off work, administrative time spent processing her time off, administrative costs for the search and training of a replacement employee if she leaves the job . . . lost profits from her decrease in output, and the increase in overtime payments to other workers who cover for her" (Day, McKenna, and Bowlus 2005, 9; Shepard and Pence 1988). One study on violence against women in Canada reported that 30 percent of reported assaults on married women led to the victims' taking time off from regular activities, and 50 percent of women who were injured took sick leave from work (Day 1995). Domestic violence, and violence against women more generally, also results in household costs, including increased healthcare expenses, the expense of replacing belongings damaged during abuse, lower income resulting from more time off work, and a loss of unpaid household production (Day, McKenna, and Bowlus 2005). A study of Canadian VAW by Greaves, Hankivsky, and Kingston-Reichers (1995) estimated that the added costs associated with tax loss from decreased incomes, police involvement, penal incarceration, legal costs, victim compensation, and relocation and self-defense costs for women added to C$4.2 billion in 1994.

Prevalence. Scholars estimate that in any given country, 20–50 percent of women have experienced physical abuse at the hands of a partner or family member (Breiding, Black, and Ryan 2008; Kapoor 2000; Tjaden and Thoennes 2000). One study indicates that 30 percent of all women who have been in a relationship have experienced physical and/or sexual violence by an intimate partner, and in the African, Eastern Mediterranean, and South Asian regions the number of women experiencing intimate-partner violence is as high as 38 percent (Garcia-Moreno and Pallitto 2013). In the United States, more than 35.6 percent of women, or almost 36.2 million, have experienced physical violence (slapping, pushing, shoving) by an intimate partner (Black et al. 2011). Further, nearly half of all women in the United States (48.4 percent) have experienced some form of psychological aggression (being called names, witnessing an intimate partner act angry in a way deemed dangerous, being insulted, being humiliated, and the like) by an intimate partner.

Honor Crimes

Honor crimes represent a subset of domestic violence, including abuse and murder, typically perpetrated by male family members against women due to actions by women that are considered to be transgressions of social norms, bringing dishonor upon the family. Such transgressions remain uncodified, but may include refusing to enter into an arranged marriage, dressing in a manner deemed unacceptable by the family, being the victim of sexual assault, seeking a divorce, committing adultery, or any unsupervised contact between a male and female that society can interpret as intimate (Amnesty International 2001; Feldner 2000; Human Rights Watch 2001). The United Nations Population Fund estimates that as many as 5,000 girls are killed each year for having "dishonored" their families (UNFPA 2000, 29). Honor killings have been reported in Bangladesh, Brazil, Ecuador, Egypt, India, Israel, Italy, Jordan, Morocco, Pakistan, Sweden, Turkey, Uganda, and the United Kingdom. Honor crimes cut across religious and cultural lines, but reports remain most prevalent in countries with a majority Muslim population (Jahangir 2000, 27).

Many scholars argue that honor crimes represent violence distinct from domestic violence because the victim-perpetrator relationship in honor crimes is often different from that in ordinary domestic violence cases. In the latter, it is less common for brothers to kill their sisters, male cousins to kill or abuse female cousins, or fathers to kill teenage daughters (Chesler 2009). Further, perpetrators typically carefully plan honor killings and the victims often receive warning a significant period ahead of time that they are at risk of being killed if they dishonor their family. Further, unlike the perpetrators of domestic violence, in some societies those committing honor crimes represent heroic avengers, which is best illustrated by the prevalence of reduced or suspended sentences for many perpetrators (ibid.). For example, in Jordan the penal code effectively reduces or eliminates punishment for honor crimes. Article 340 states that "he who catches his wife or one of his female unlawfuls committing adultery with another, and kills, wounds, of injures one or both of them, is exempted from any penalty" (Abu-Odeh 2011, 4). In Jordan in 1999, a male perpetrator raped Amal, a seventeen-year-old. Amal became pregnant following the rape, and family members viewed her experience as dishonoring to the family. After a failed attempt by Amal's father and brother to kill her by gunshot, her father received no sentence for the crime and her brother received a seven-year prison sentence, reduced from the minimum fourteen-year sentence mandated under Jordanian law (Arnold 2001, 1345). In another example, from 1994, the brother of Kifaya Husayn, a 16-year-old Jordanian girl, killed Kifaya to "cleanse his honor" after she was raped by another brother (Feldner 2000, 41).

Women living under the threat of becoming victims of honor crimes face significant danger, and other forms of violence against women contribute to the prevalence of honor crimes. For example, a woman experiencing domestic violence in marriage may choose to stay in the marriage and hope the abuse ends, rather than leave the marriage and hope that her husband or another male family member does not kill her (Human Rights Watch 2001). Further, as the cases of Amal and Kifaya illustrate, honor crimes can occur when family members perceive female rape victims as bringing shame or dishonor on the family (Human Rights Watch 2001; Feldner 2000). Rape victims may also face grave risk for reporting rape in societies where honor crimes are prevalent. In one case, the relatives of Arbab Khatoon murdered her after she reported to police that she was raped in the Jacobabad district of Pakistan. She was reportedly killed for bringing dishonor upon her family as a result of going to the police (Amnesty International 2001, 8).

MARITAL RAPE

Defined. Marital (or spousal) rape is a form of domestic violence in which rape occurs in the context of a marriage or de facto marital relationship. Marital rape represents a form of sexual intimate-partner violence in which a woman is physically forced to have sexual intercourse against her will or because she is afraid of what her partner might do (Garcia-Moreno and Pallitto 2013). The tactics used to force intimate partners to submit to sexual acts include nonphysical sexual coercion, which includes social or normative coercion, and interpersonal coercion. Social and normative coercion involve the use of tradition and norms, including societal conceptions of a wifely duty to satisfy her husband, despite her potentially conflicting desires. Interpersonal coercion involves the husband's use of resources or economic power to compel his wife to fulfill his sexual demands (Finkelhor and Yllo 1985). The husband may also threaten or force sex on his wife through violence.

Causes. Feminist scholars argue that marital rape represents a tool for men to exert social control over women through the use of the patriarchal familial relationships. Legal precedent rooted in "unities theory" (developed in seventeenth-century England) espoused the legality of overt male social control in the familial relationship. This theoretical paradigm argued that husband and wife become one entity when they are married and that the woman suspends her legal rights during marriage, while the husband regards her as his property

(Blackstone 1765). Similar gender-role expectations are espoused in various religiously oriented institutions as well. As a result of patriarchal traditions within the family, many in society perceive sexual violence by an intimate partner to be a less severe violation of women's rights than stranger or date rape—so much so that in many countries' legal systems, marital rape often does not constitute rape (Auster and Leone 2001; Frese, Moya, and Megias 2004).

Consequences. Studies find numerous adverse consequences of marital rape on both individuals and society. One study indicates that one in ten women in the United States has been raped by an intimate partner (Black et al. 2011). Another survey finds that 36.2 percent of women raped by an intimate partner sustained an injury (other than the rape itself) (CDC 2003). The costs and consequences associated with marital rape correlate with those related to domestic violence, specifically the individual mental and physical health costs, as well as societal social and economic costs. For example, one study reports that in the United States, 14.8 percent of those surveyed experienced an injury and 10 percent missed at least one day of work or school as a result of intimate-partner violence, including rape (Black et al. 2011). The same study finds a higher-than-average prevalence of frequent headaches, chronic pain, difficulty sleeping, and activity limitations among women with a history of intimate-partner violence, including rape. In fact, the percentage of women who rated their physical and mental health as poor was about three times greater among victims of intimate-partner violence than among those with no history of this form of violence (Black et al. 2011, 62).

Women also face adverse reproductive and perinatal health effects from marital rape, including unintended pregnancies and sexually transmitted diseases. Further, women living in a dangerous environment face high stress, which adversely influences maternal health as well as birth weight. Various studies find that intimate-partner violence is positively related to low birth weight and preterm birth (Garcia-Moreno and Pallitto 2013, 23)

Prevalence. One study finds that approximately 11.1 million women in the United States has been raped by an intimate partner in her lifetime, and an estimated 686,000 women in the United States indicated that they had been raped by an intimate partner in the year prior to taking the survey (Black et al. 2011). One WHO study reported that the proportion of female victims of marital rape ranged from 4 percent in Serbia and Montenegro to 46 percent in Bangladesh and Ethiopia, with nearly one-third of Ethiopian women reporting having been physically forced into sexual intercourse within the twelve months preceding the survey (WHO 2005).

The reluctance of governments to provide legal recourse for female victims of marital rape contributes to its high prevalence. Until 1977, women in the United States had no legal recourse to rape by their spouses (Whatley 1993). In Nepal, victims of marital rape had no access to justice until 2002, when the Supreme Court found that "sexual intercourse in conjugal life is a normal course of behavior, which must be based on consent. No religion may ever take it [marital rape] as lawful because the aim of a good religion is not to hate or cause loss to anyone" (United Nations Entity 2012). The Supreme Court ordered parliament to amend the rape law, but the penalty for marital rape in Nepal was set at only six months' imprisonment, much lower than for other forms of sexual assault (ibid.).

Conclusion

As this chapter has highlighted, violence against women represents a global pandemic, one with various adverse individual and societal consequences. In the following chapters we focus primarily on societal (state) solutions to the problem of violence against women: strong legal protections from violence. We present various hypotheses related to the adoption and strength of legal guarantees addressing the four forms of violence discussed in this chapter, and examine them using an original dataset on the presence and strength of legal protections.

CHAPTER 2

POLITICAL, ECONOMIC, AND SOCIAL DETERMINANTS OF DOMESTIC GENDER-BASED-VIOLENCE POLICY

To address the pandemic of violence against women (VAW) globally, it is important to focus on multiple levels of causal factors, including individual characteristics, the relationship between the victim and perpetrator of violence, the community, and society. Given that VAW represents a violation of women's human rights, the state has a primary responsibility to address it. The state often addresses human rights violations through the use of legal mechanisms; that is, legally prohibiting human rights violations at the international and domestic levels. As a result, in order to assess state efforts to address VAW, it is important to understand the factors that influence the adoption and strength of VAW legal protections.

In this chapter, we elaborate on *domestic* political, economic, and social or cultural explanations for the strength and enforcement of legal protections against gender-based violence. Many of these factors have been expounded on in the vast literature addressing gender-based violence. However, our data allow us not only to examine the relationship between these various mechanisms in the domestic adoption and enforcement of legal guarantees, but also to make generalizations regarding the importance of these mechanisms across countries for the protection of women from violence. Our analyses also lend themselves to various policy recommendations in the global effort to reduce and eliminate VAW.

What Political Factors Influence the Adoption and Strength of VAW Legal Protections?

Women's Political Participation

What role do female representatives play in the strength and enforcement of national legal protections related to violence against women? Since the call for greater access to public office for women in the Beijing Platform (the platform for action concluding the Fourth World Conference on Women in Beijing, China, in 1995), the presence of women in representative office has increased substantially. The global average percentage of women in parliament increased from 9 percent in 1995 to 16 percent in 2004. However, sixteen countries show that women represent 30 percent or more of parliament (UNRISD 2005). In fact, Rwanda achieved extraordinary levels of female representation in 2003, when almost half of all members of parliament were women. However, the number of women in politics worldwide remains low. As a result, many countries are adopting affirmative-action platforms to boost the number of female representatives, including the use of quotas and seat reservations, among others (UNRISD 2005). However, the extent to which these increased numbers influence women's interests is highly debated.

Some scholars argue that female representatives have a relatively large and important influence on policymaking, particularly in their representation of women and women's issues. Various studies find that female legislators are more likely than male legislators to introduce bills that address issues related to women's rights (Dodson and Carroll 1991; Firestone 1995; Kathlene 1994; McAllister and Studlar 1992; Norris 1996; Vega and Firestone 1995; Thomas 1991). There are two basic arguments used to explain the ways in which women in government represent the interests of women. *Descriptive representation* arguments highlight the characteristics of representatives; that is, a female elected official represents women simply by her presence in office. *Substantive representation* arguments focus on the actions taken by female representatives while in office (Pitkin 1967). Representation is often rooted in group identity and shared interests (Phillips 1998). Women as a group share various life experiences in the home, workplace, and public sphere, which causes them to "prioritize and express different types of values, attitudes, and policy priorities" (Lovenduski and Norris 2003, 87).[1] A woman in government is thought to represent women if "by her opinions and/or actions, she sustains the wishes, needs or interests of the female population, which are deemed women's issues" (Tremblay 1998, 439). Women's issues may encompass both feminist and traditional issues ascribed to women, including issues involving equal pay for equal work, reproductive rights, violence against women, family, children, and education (Dodson and Carroll 1991; Saint-Germain 1989).

Empirical evidence provides some support for the idea that women represent women's issues in the legislature. Thomas (1994, 151) finds that women, on average, introduce and pass 0.35 more initiatives associated with women's issues than do men. Studies have also pointed to the importance of a tipping point. One such study examining US states found that in legislatures composed of less than 10 percent women, female representatives were less likely to initiate legislation related to women's issues (legislation related to women, children, and the family), while women in legislatures composed of more than 10 percent women were much more likely (Thomas 1994; Welch and Thomas 1991).

However, a second group of scholars argues quite the opposite; that is, that female elected officials do not represent issues of concern to women in office for various reasons. Beteta (2006) presents a number of reasons that women in parliament may not be politically effective, particularly regarding women's issues. First, in developing countries women's access to politics is often determined by elite family connections, not by experience or participation in a women's movement (Reynolds 1999). Weldon (2002) argues that the presence of women in government alone does not influence policy related to violence against women, but must be accompanied by a strong, autonomous women's movement. More specifically, Weldon (97) asserts that an autonomous women's movement is important to "magnify the influence of a women's caucus or a women's cabinet, and provide an external base of support and legitimacy to counterbalance internal government resistance to the enactment or implementation of feminist policies." Second, political parties often consider feminists an electoral liability, which in turn decreases the likelihood of women promoting feminist concerns while in office (UNRISD 2005). In countries where this is the case, women in politics often remain uninvolved in women's organizations and those that are active feminists likely lose out early in a race (UNRISD 2005). This means that women's issues, including violence against women, may not be of primary concern for women elected to government. Finally, gender-specific issues may be subordinate to other issues as a result of women's class, political party, and other identities (Vijayalakshmi 2002). Many women do not believe that their identity as women is their most important one. In fact, Weldon (2002, 71) argues that "the central question for feminist theory over the past decade has been how the group 'women' can be seen as politically relevant in itself, when class, race, ethnic, and other differences significantly divide women."[2]

Given these arguments and the mixed theoretical and empirical record associated with women's representation, it is difficult to determine the effect of female policymakers on the strength and enforcement of legal protections against gender-based violence. However, we argue that women's political participation, whether through formal participation in office or activity in women's organizations, gives women an *opportunity* to voice issues that directly influence women, such as gender-based violence. Weldon (2002) argues that an autonomous women's movement is necessary to pressure the government into policy change. As a result, the presence of women's organizations and pro-women's-rights activists likely generates public support and pressure to adopt stronger legislation. In other words, the probability of VAW emerging on the national policy agenda rises.

Civil Conflict

What role does civil conflict have on violence against women? Gender-based violence during and following conflict is gaining attention on the international stage as a human rights violation. Specifically, rape has been framed as a weapon or tactic of warfare since the founding of the International Criminal Court (ICC) and the war-crimes tribunals. In fact, the Rome Statute of the ICC recognizes gender-based violence, including rape, sexual slavery, forced prostitution, forced pregnancy, forced sterilization, and gender-based persecutions, as crimes against humanity and war crimes. Further, the United Nations placed the issue of gender-based violence during armed conflict on its agenda with the passage of UN Security Council Resolution 1325 on women, peace, and security in 2000, and Resolution 1820 in 2008, which focuses on rape as a weapon of war and sexual violence as a threat to international peace and security.

Women's human rights are often violated during peacetime, but such violations, including gender-based violence, are magnified during times of conflict. Rape has been used as a weapon of war or a means of ethnic cleansing, as was the case in the former Yugoslavia. Serbian forces raped Muslim and Croat women in an attempt to create more Serbs to fuel Serbian nationalism and create more soldiers to defend the country through reproduction (Salzman 2006). In the eastern Democratic Republic of the Congo (DRC), the Democratic Forces for the Liberation of Rwanda have used rape as a weapon of war, including gang rape, in response to government policies. Similarly, Congolese army soldiers have used rape as a weapon to punish women and girls perceived to be collaborating with the opposition (Woudenberg 2012). Rape as a weapon of war is not unique to those countries; combatants during the genocide in Rwanda and

Russian soldiers in WWII also used rape as a tool in battle (the latter to punish German women) (ibid.). In a landmark decision following the use of rape as a weapon of war in the former Yugoslavia, the International Criminal Tribunal for the former Yugoslavia ruled in 2001 that rape and sexual enslavement represent crimes against humanity.

Violence against women during conflict may also be used to inhibit women's ability to contribute to the community. Raping, injuring, or killing women can damage the community's ability to function, particularly where women are responsible for much of the economic activity, including agricultural labor or production of resources (True 2012). VAW not only hinders women's economic capacity, but also inhibits their ability to conceive children, which may curtail births within a particular group (Salzman 2006). Also, societal discrimination against female rape victims often results in the rejection of a rape victim by her family; a woman's husband may abandon her, leaving her little chance of marrying again, and she may even be ostracized from the community (Williams 2012; Niarchos 2006).

Further, due to traditional gender divisions, male members of the military or militia may view gender-based violence as a way to fulfill their sense of entitlement as men (True 2012). The military often develops patriarchal notions of "man as protector" and propagates "notions of male sexuality and virility" (Niarchos 2006, 290). Research shows that male justifications for gender-based violence are often "crafted out of statist norms around heterosexuality and masculinity produced within their society's military institutions and armed forces" (Eriksson Baaz and Stern 2009, 514). During times of civil conflict, gender inequalities often intensify, and those in power, mainly men, can more easily resort to gender-based violence (True 2012). Woudenberg (2012, 133) makes this argument clearly with respect to the DRC: "Congolese women . . . have always been seen as inferior to men, but the society has now been so extremely brutalized that social norms which used to protect women and girls have been completely eroded."

Gender-based violence certainly intensifies during civil conflict; however, post-conflict societies witness high levels of gender-based violence as well. Conflict leaves many women as heads of household as they are widowed or abandoned. Households headed by women face significant poverty and vulnerability to continued violence (Williams 2012). Further, in post-conflict situations, women often enter into refugee camps and become susceptible to gender-based violence, living in extremely close quarters in often-inhospitable conditions with thousands of other people (ibid.).[3] The impunity related to gender-based violence during conflict influences attitudes regarding the social acceptability of violence following conflict. Empirical evidence indicates a "greater presence of domestic violence, sexual violence and abuse associated with transnational sex in refugee and internationally displaced person camps, forced pregnancy and marriage, and trafficking for prostitution" (True 2012, 136).

Political and economic instability (particularly as the new government is designed and implemented) during and following conflict produces a climate of impunity, one in which legal implementation and law enforcement are particularly ineffective. Walter (1997) argues that civil wars produce a particularly unstable environment, as warring groups find it difficult to credibly commit to disarmament, resulting in repeated bargaining failures. Instability makes the legal system particularly ineffective. For example, in 2006 the parliament of the DRC adopted a new law on sexual violence, broadening the definition of rape and increasing penalties for the crime—but in an environment facing instability and vast impunity, "implementation of the new laws and policies has lagged" (Woudenberg 2012, 135) in addressing sexual violence.

What Economic Factors Influence the Adoption and Strength of VAW Legal Protections?

Micro-Level Economic Factors: Women's Economic Rights

Scholars attribute various micro- and macro-level economic factors to high levels of violence against women. In fact, many claim that empowerment and education are vital for women to remove themselves from violence experienced in the home or in public. Studies show that greater gender inequality in development is associated with higher levels of VAW, and scholars highlight a robust relationship between access to resources (such as land, income, property, employment, and education) and VAW (Remenyi 2007). As women gain access to employment, education, and economic rights in general, they establish relationships outside the home. This allows them to more easily gain practical and emotional support, providing them with more opportunities to escape violence (Johnson, Ollus, and Nevala 2008; UN Women 2012). Women with an alternative social network (through employment or other organizational involvement outside the home) become less socially isolated and may be more likely to discuss and even report experiences of violence (Renzetti 2011).

Further, when women are in a position of economic dependence on male partners, they have less control in the relationship and fewer options to communicate their experiences and report violence against them (Kalmuss and Strauss 1982; Levinson 1989; Postmus et. al 2009). They may feel trapped, with little opportunity to escape. In fact, between 25 and 50 percent of intimate-partner-violence victims experience some type of housing problem when trying to end an abusive relationship, and many women become homeless as a result of leaving an abusive partner (Baker, Cook, and Norris 2003). With increased decision-making power in the home, women can more easily remove themselves from situations of violence. True (2012, 31) states, "The strict division of roles in the domestic sphere constrains women's public participation and their access to education and economic opportunities in the market, in turn creating hierarchical structures that entrap many women into potentially violent environments at home and at work." Greater access to resources, including capital, land, property, and loans, enhances women's ability to support themselves, and their potential to leave a violent environment.

Empirical evidence also indicates that women with greater economic decision-making power within the home, often through increased income, make different financial allocation decisions than men. Income in the hands of women results in greater improvements in child health and a larger share of income spent on nutrients, health, and housing (Duflo 2003; Rubalcava, Teruel, and Thomas 2009; Thomas 1990 and 1992). These findings have led to an increase in microcredit and microfinance by various organizations, which are largely restricted to women. These small loans are designed to provide women with decision-making power over the household income, which may influence the allocation of spent income and potentially development and health. Once women are empowered through greater economic and educational opportunities, they are increasingly likely to mobilize around ending VAW, and one solution is to press for stronger legal protections against violence.

Still, other scholars present an opposing argument, claiming that increased economic opportunities (employment, education, access to resources) for women result in increased levels of violence. Women's economic opportunities are viewed as a threat to male dominance, which may lead to increased violence as men attempt to maintain control and authority (Heise and Garcia-Moreno 2002; Jewkes 2002). Anecdotal evidence of this comes from South Asia, where greater economic and educational opportunities for women are correlated with an increase in acid attacks. However, despite these arguments, existing evidence shows a strong positive correlation, on average, between economic opportunities for women and various UN indicators of gender equality.

Macro-Level Economic Factors: Trade Liberalization

Various macroeconomic factors arguably explain variation in policy and practice related to violence against women. Economic globalization and its accompanying neoliberal economic-policy reforms, such as liberalized trade, deregulation, and privatization, uniquely affect women in society. There are two schools of thought regarding the way economic globalization, particularly trade liberalization, influences violence against women, and women's rights more generally. First, some scholars argue that economic globalization creates an environment in which advancements in women's rights become increasingly likely. Trade liberalization often results in an increase in export-oriented and labor-intensive production, particularly in developing countries where labor is abundant (and capital is relatively scarce). Capital-abundant (developed) countries, where labor is often scarce, search for cheaper sources of labor as well as an economic environment characterized by deregulation and tax breaks for firms. Economic growth and development increase due to income gains and the reduction in the prices of imported goods following trade liberalization. These gains are beneficial, particularly for those possessing the abundant factor of production (which is labor in most developing countries) (Bhagwati 2004; Milner and Kubota 2005; Rogowski 1987). In many developing countries women disproportionately possess the abundant factor of production (labor), and therefore are more likely to accrue the benefits of trade. Trade liberalization, and economic globalization in general, generate gains in women's economic opportunities in the formal labor market, which increases their participation in the public sphere, access to education, and employment opportunities. Given that some of the primary causes of violence against women are women's lack of economic opportunities, economic dependence on male family members, and lack of education, increased participation by women in the labor market, generated by a rise in economic globalization, arguably places women in a position where they are less vulnerable to violence. Employment and education opportunities and the subsequent rise in income provides women with greater bargaining power in the home and allows them to renegotiate the gendered household division of labor (Richards and Gelleny 2007; True 2012).

Mosely and Uno (2007) argue that trade liberalization is associated with fewer economic rights (as discussed later), but that foreign direct investment (FDI) is positively related with rights as investors often bring best practices for worker rights to host countries. When foreign direct investors' primarily focus on the production of goods closer to particular markets rather than reducing costs, investors care more about finding quality labor, which may lead them to "expend resources on employee training and benefits, and pay higher wages to reduce turnover" (ibid., 926). As a result, economic globalization, particularly FDI, arguably provides greater economic opportunities for women and improves their status in society (Acker 2004; Deo 2006; Gray, Kittilson, and Sandholtz 2006).

However, a second school of thought argues that while economic globalization may generate economic growth, its benefits are unequally distributed throughout society, with women receiving little benefit from the economic policies that accompany economic globalization. For example, as capital becomes increasingly mobile, scholars argue that investors can threaten exit, resulting in a race to the bottom with respect to tax, labor and wage standards, and social services (Crotty, Epstein, and Kelly 1998; Drezner 2001; Eichengreen 1997; Garrett 1998; Rodrik 1998). In other words, multinational corporations often opt to create subcontracting relationships with firms in other countries to decrease costs, and "a nation's ability to produce a good at the lowest possible cost is central to increasing export share and to winning business for local subcontracting firms" (Mosely and Uno 2007, 928).

This race to the bottom disproportionately affects women because many industries searching for cheap labor employ women, often young migrant women from rural areas of the country, which results in the "feminization of poverty" (Chen et al. 2005; Peterson 2003). In fact, in export-intensive industries such as textiles, footwear, and food processing, 80 percent of the workers are women (True 2012, 81). Developing countries often establish export processing zones in an effort to adhere to the demands for lower-cost production by firms. These zones focus on manufacturing for export and often involve labor-intensive, low-skill work as well as restrictions on labor rights (Mosely and Uno 2007). Further, reduction or elimination of tariffs and tax breaks forces governments to look for alternative forms of revenue, which often results in cutbacks to or the elimination of social services, which are often disproportionately used by women (Bergeron 2001; Hemmati and Gardiner 2002; Pearson 2003; Rao and Kelleher 2005). Moseley and Uno (2007, 928) argue that the race to the bottom is particularly prevalent with respect to trade openness as a form of economic globalization as "firms can reduce demands for wages and nonwage benefits by restricting collective labor rights; government can further serve investors' interests by not providing or not enforcing these rights."

How does this environment influence violence against women? First, low wages and labor standards brought by companies looking for cheap labor, as well a lack of regulation, increases violence in the workplace, particularly abuse of reproductive rights, sexual harassment, rape, and sexual assault (True 2012, 77). Women experiencing violence in the workplace are often afraid to report it to authorities because they fear losing their jobs given the overabundance of labor in many developing countries and the potential for firms with mobile capital to threaten exit from a country (Karega 2002). Additionally, as more women enter the formal economy, men's "breadwinner" or "provider" identity is challenged in the home, which may result in men using violence against women to reaffirm their dominance (Kersten 1996; True 2012, 31).

True (2012, 33) states, "Globalization has . . . expanded women's formal economic participation, while leaving unchanged the underlying patriarchal structures that perpetuate women's inequality with men and their susceptibility to violence." Some research even indicates that as women gain economic opportunities, gender-based violence increases (Heise and Garcia-Moreno 2002). The perpetuation of social structures that discriminate against women, as a result of economic globalization, make policy reform and enforcement of gender-based-violence legislation unlikely.

What Cultural or Societal Factors Influence the Adoption and Strength of VAW Legal Protections?

Societal Discrimination

Culture and society play a role in violence against women. Culture has been defined broadly as "a core of traditional ideas, practices, and technology shared by a people" (Conway, Ahern, and Steurnagel 1995, 2). Weldon (2002, 34) claims culture may encompass many different indicators, including "social institutions, the role of women in the family, and the economic conditions of women." Some cultural practices directly result in violence against women. Consider the case of dowry violence, where a bride brings money, goods, or property into a marriage and often the bride's family makes payments to the groom's family. Societal pressure to marry daughters may result in vulnerable women ending up in abusive marriages, and facing beating, starvation, and burning, among other forms of violence. Other cultural practices are directly associated with violence against women, including female genital mutilation, forced marriage, honor crimes, and forced sterilization.[4]

Cultural attitudes not only influence the level of violence against women in society, but also likely influence policymaking, including the adoption and enforcement of legislation related to VAW. Gender-based violence is a cross-cultural phenomenon; that is, it occurs across all societies and within all cultural traditions. Rape, marital rape, domestic violence, and sexual harassment, among various other forms, are not limited to a specific region or group of people (Watts and Zimmerman 2002).

By analyzing cultural factors as explanations of violence against women, we risk stereotyping the treatment of women within specific cultures. Further, we risk "essentializing" those cultures: "underestimating differences among people in culture and supporting racist discourses that construct members of minority groups, or other non-Western nations, as a homogenous 'other'" (Fontes and McCloskey 2011). The risk involves omitting *agency* or the complex and contested identity of particular groups. Some scholars argue that essentialism does not grasp the complexities of the social world and conflicts with women's rights and women's-rights movements (MacKinnon 2000). The failure to grasp the contextual differences among various actors can lead to the improper specification of solutions to issues such as VAW. Kapur (2005, 20) notes this problem in stating, "Postcolonialism understands that historical wrongs and traumas are not resolved, healed, or brought to closure simply through reformist projects, apologies, or reparations. What is important to interrogate and understand is how colonial histories discursively suffuse the postcolonial present so overtly."

The lack of universal solutions to the problem of VAW calls into question the role of the state in resolving these problems. Merry and Shimmin (2011) argue that the recognition of domestic violence as a human rights violation remains contentious in the United States, largely as a result of a complex neoliberal understanding. More specifically, neoliberal understanding of welfare "insists that needy and dependent individuals take responsibility for themselves . . . battered women become safe by achieving self-sufficiency and autonomy . . . by making choices and avoiding dependence on a partner or the state" (113–114). The United States faces this particular challenge, rooted in historical contextual issues, to reducing and eliminating domestic violence, while other countries face different challenges to finding solutions (policy or otherwise) to the problem of VAW.

However, only by engaging in this dialogue can we hope to institute structural and social change with respect to the reduction or elimination of VAW. Spivak (1988) echoes this view through the development of a concept called "strategic essentialism," which recognizes that claims about women and women's rights are generalizations of reality, intended to achieve certain policy outcomes and not to be statements about "apolitical depictions of reality" (295). Young (1997; 2000), similarly, argues that women are not a single group with a shared identity, but instead represent a structural social group, emerging as a result of similar social norms and institutions that produce a distinct perspective on politics and policy. Further, studying VAW as a human rights violation grants leverage to those wishing to make generalizations by focusing on structural inequalities and seeking "solutions through structural change such as new government policies, reductions in poverty, and enhancements to individual coping strategies" (Merry and Shimmin 2011, 114).

Strategic essentialism is important for generating policy change. Many scholars claim that reforms must be rooted in the existing practices and culture if they are to be accepted (An-Na'im 1992; Mahmood 2005; Merry 2006). Only by examining the various facets through which culture contributes to human rights violations, including violence against women, can we begin to propose context-specific reform proposals for reducing or eliminating VAW.

Although scholars have yet to pinpoint the exact mechanism at work in the relationship between culture and policy outcomes, Weldon (2002, 35) claims, "few would deny that social practices, cultural attitudes, and institutions have some effect on policymaking." Merry (2006) provides various examples of the role of cultural factors in inhibiting the adoption of legislation and enforcement of legal guarantees related to gender-based violence. She examines the reluctance of police and courts in Fiji to investigate, prosecute, and convict perpetrators of violence against women as an example of cultural or societal factors contributing to a lack of enforcement of legal guarantees related to gender-based violence. She notes, "A 1988 study of the Suva area found that police reconcile 64 percent of the reported cases of domestic violence, generally by persuading wives to drop the charges. . . . Both police and courts find these cases embarrassing and often do not support women who complain" (144). The societal discrimination variable included in our original dataset is intended to capture the influence of the social acceptance of abuse against women, including cultural, traditional, or customary practices that discriminate against women, on the likelihood of observing strong gender-based violence legislation.

Religious Institutions

Religion, particularly religious institutions and practices, represents a specific feature of society related to VAW and VAW-related policy (Narayan 1997; Weldon 2002). Religious institutions represent hierarchical structures, much like other governmental and nongovernmental organizations. As such, the religious elites, acting within institutions, seek to maintain their position of authority and are not immune from advocating norms and ideas that may be harmful to a particular group of people in society.

Many religious institutions place women in a subordinate position in the home and society, which subsequently reduces their social and economic opportunities outside the home. For example, traditional Islamic law affords women highly unequal status in society. In fact, Arzt (1990) states with respect to women under Islamic law,

> Women are legally disqualified from holding general political or judicial office, and within the family they lack the capacity to initiate a marriage contract or obtain a unilateral divorce. By law their inheritance of property is usually about half the share of a male with the same degree of relationship to the deceased. Husbands have the right to chastise their wives for "disobedience," including by "light beating." Muslim women can leave the home to seek employment not to fulfill personal ambitions but only when they lack all other means of support. Moreover, a woman's testimony in court is worth only one-half of a man's testimony. (208)

With respect to the Islamic religious tradition, some scholars argue that the Qur'an was initially considered a source of enhanced women's rights, including status and dignity, but "the influence of social conditions and the interpretation of many diverse cultural traditions led to the inferior status of women being written into Islamic law" (Mayer 2013, 114). Religious texts, as interpreted by various institutional elites and advocated and applied to the public sphere, can create an environment in which rights are largely removed. Mayer (25) argues,

> The most serious and pervasive human rights problems afflicting the Middle East are not ones created by the increasingly rare survival of intact traditional cultures; they are ones created by governmental policies and laws inimical to rights and democratic freedoms—and in the case of Islamic human rights schemes, by policies and laws that are designed by elites for implementation by modern state systems at the expense of rights and freedoms of the individual.

Within the Islamic religious institutional tradition, the subordinate status of women plays a role in the level of VAW in society. In the Middle East, fewer women work outside the home and hold positions in government than in any other region of the world. Many scholars claim that this anomaly is a result of the region's Islamic traditions (Sharabi 1988; World Bank 2004). Participation in the labor force allows women to work jobs that bring them into contact with each other and to share information with one another, lowers barriers to collective action, enables development of social networks, and provides women with greater access to information about health and contraception (Amin et al. 1998; Kabeer and Mahmud 2004). Conservative Islamic religious institutions assert that women should not work outside the home and employment should involve jobs related only to women and children (Mayer 2013, 116). Segregation from labor markets impedes women's political and social influence and, as examined earlier with respect to women's economic rights, has a detrimental influence on VAW.

The empirical record of the relationship between Christianity and violence against women is mixed. Weldon (2002, 43) finds that on average, countries that are primarily Protestant are positively associated with the number of government policies addressing violence against women; however, this relationship is not statistically significant. Other research indicates that members of conservative Protestant denominations and individuals who embrace strict views of the Bible tend to prefer traditional (patriarchal) gender roles (Hertel and Hughes 1987; Peek, Lowe, and Williams 1991). Such views have led some scholars to argue that conservative theology may increase intimate-partner violence (Nason-Clark 1997; Scanzoni and Arnett 1987). Others argue that Christianity and Protestantism decrease levels of domestic violence and that religious attendance and devotion are positively related with marital quality (Dudley and Kosinski 1990; Hansen 1987).

In later chapters we examine the relationship between religious institutions (majority-Muslim and majority-Christian countries) and VAW-related policy. Undoubtedly, the vast differences within Islamic religious institutions and Christian religious institutions warrant further examination in the study of VAW-related policy and likely provide fruitful avenues for future research. However, various scholars point to the role of religious institutions in human rights, and women's rights more specifically, so in this book we focus broadly on the prevalence of religious institutions cross-nationally.

Do Domestic Legal Guarantees Influence VAW-Related Outcomes?

Women's Health

In addition to examining the influence of various factors on the strength of legal guarantees, we explore the influence of domestic gender-based violence legal protections on VAW. Many scholars argue that gender-based violence has a negative effect on women's health, both short and long term. In fact, empirical evidence shows that women who have experienced violence are more likely to develop recurring physical and mental health problems than those who have not experienced violence (Caldwell and Redecker 2005; Campbell 2002; Coker 2007; Macy, Ferron, and Crosby 2009). VAW can have direct and indirect effects on women's health, including injuries resulting from violent encounters, physical health problems as a result of fear, stress, and other psychological consequences of violence (Campbell 2002; Kendall-Tackett 2007; Macy, Ermentrout, and Johns 2011), "chronic pain, headaches and migraines, memory loss, abdominal pain, gastrointestinal problems, gynecological problems, as well as mental health problems, such as depression, alcohol and drug abuse, low self-esteem, fear, anxiety, post-traumatic stress disorder, and suicide attempts" (Johnson, Ollus, and Nevala 2008, 67).

Although strong domestic legal guarantees do not translate directly into outcomes, we argue that countries that adopt policies protecting women from violence (especially when those policies are enforced) are more likely to have lower levels of women's physical health problems than are countries that have not adopted such policies.

Women's Status

We argue that various indicators of women's status will improve as domestic gender-based violence law and enforcement rise.[5] The adoption of legal guarantees is an indicator of the societal acceptance of violence against women as a public, rather than a private or family, problem. Legal protections provide police and prosecutors with tools to bring justice for the victims of violence. The evolution of legal guarantees and adoption of more comprehensive laws, as well as improved enforcement efforts, help guarantee that cases of gender-based violence are pursued and investigated, and that prosecutions are made, which is an important step in protecting women from violence.

Criminalization and enforcement efforts generally require countries to "develop and pass laws against gender violence, train police to arrest offenders, encourage no-drop (i.e., mandated) prosecution, and train judges to treat wife battering and sexual assault seriously" (Merry 2006, 139). Consider, as an example, reform to domestic violence laws in the United States in the 1990s. Prior to those reforms, women's rights advocates presented a series of lawsuits in response to police failure to protect women from violence, particularly as a result of police advocating a "take a walk around the block and cool off response" (Goodmark 2011, 192). Women's rights advocates argued that mandatory arrests would remove police discretion as a factor in arrest decisions. Further, instituting no-drop policies for prosecutors meant the law required authorities to pursue cases, regardless of victim willingness. As legal guarantees have evolved, protections have increased and enforcement efforts have grown, and "the belief that the legal system is best placed to respond to domestic violence has become a cultural norm" (Goodmark 2012, 4).

Legal guarantees protecting women from violence are expanding to include other forms of abuse. For example, India's Protection of Women from Domestic Violence Act covers economic abuse, as does legislation in other countries where economic dependence often contributes to violence, including Cambodia, Ecuador, and Zimbabwe. Expanding national laws to include economic abuse may "provide women with options beyond abusive relationships, help to stabilize the country, and enable women to escape some of this violence" (Goodmark 2011, 206). Legal guarantees coupled with economic opportunities for women are likely to have a strong positive influence on reducing and eliminating violence (Gupta 2010; True 2012).

Enforcement of gender-based-violence laws is also crucial for improving the status of women. In countries where women do not expect legal guarantees to be enforced, it is plausible that they are unlikely to utilize the legal system to bring perpetrators of violence to justice. Further, perpetrators of violence are likely to be further deterred by the law when it is generally enforced. Merry (2006, 139) states, in reference to gender-violence laws, "because implementation of laws lags well behind the passage of these laws, activists devote considerable energy to implementation strategies." While it is not the final step in eliminating or reducing violence against women, we expect that the adoption and enforcement of comprehensive legal guarantees related to violence against women reduces the level of violence and improves the status of women in society.

Conclusion

We've explored the theoretical foundations for various domestic political, economic, and social factors associated with violence against women. We posit that many of these factors, including women's political participation, civil conflict, women's economic rights, economic globalization, societal discrimination, and religious institutions influence the strength and enforcement of gender-based violence legal guarantees. In the chapters to follow, we present an original dataset on cross-national legal guarantees, enforcement, and societal discrimination related to violence against women. We then empirically examine these hypotheses and explore the policy implications of these findings.

The following is a list of hypotheses generated by this chapter's topics. First come the hypotheses we test in this book, and second are hypotheses that may be interesting for future research.

Hypotheses Tested in This Book

- Countries with higher levels of women's political participation are more likely than others to adopt legal guarantees protecting women from violence.
- Countries involved in violent civil conflict are less likely to enforce legal guarantees related to gender-based violence.
- Countries with greater economic rights for women are more likely to adopt legal guarantees addressing gender-based violence.
- To the extent that countries have liberalized trade, domestic laws that protect women from gender-based violence should be less prevalent around the world.
- Countries with higher levels of societal discrimination are less likely to adopt legal guarantees addressing gender-based violence.
- Majority-Muslim and majority-Christian countries are less likely to adopt strong legal guarantees addressing gender-based violence.
- In countries with stronger legal guarantees related to gender-based violence, women are less likely to have physical health problems.
- As the strength of legal guarantees related to gender-based violence rises, the status of women rises.

Hypotheses Needing Further Research

- Countries with greater educational opportunities for women are more likely to adopt legal guarantees addressing gender-based violence.
- Countries with greater levels of foreign direct investment are more likely to adopt legal guarantees addressing gender-based violence.
- As the strength of legal guarantees related to gender-based violence rises, the status of women rises in countries with relatively greater economic rights for women.

CHAPTER 3

❧

LEGAL FRAMEWORKS

The main focus of this book is a global investigation of legal frameworks that tackle the problem of violence against women (VAW): how and why they vary from country to country and what effects, if any, they have on the lives of women in those countries. One major assumption is that, despite its well-publicized lack of enforcement mechanisms, international law accomplishes its goals to some reasonable extent. More specifically, by establishing both norms and binding legal obligations, we expect international law to lay the foundation for the enactment of domestic legislation aimed at reducing gender-based violence.

These expectations give no certainty, however. Feminists have long written about the discrepancy in law's treatment of what happens in the private versus public spheres of life as being one deficiency (among others) in law's ability to address gender inequalities; perhaps law reifies inequalities. This argument goes that violence against women is dominantly experienced in the private sphere, yet international law classically has regulated the public rather than the private (see, e.g., Edwards 2011; MacKinnon 2006; Saguy 2003; Ulrich 2000). Yet law increasingly has taken notice of the private/public distinction, and there is some reason to believe that domestic legal incorporation of international norms may yield benefits. A 1999 study by the Office of the High Commissioner for Human Rights investigated the impact of six human rights treaties on actual enjoyment of these rights in twenty countries. One of the key findings was that "the international system has had its greatest impact where treaty norms have been made part of domestic law" (Heyns and Viljoen 2001, 487).

There are, of course, many reasons to be skeptical of politics and government, as well as the power of law to affect positive social change such as elimination of entrenched inequalities. Brown (1995, 131) notes that MacKinnon's style of feminist jurisprudence aimed at "employing rights discourse to expose and redress inequalities" is certainly not without its critiques and critics. Again, however, it may be possible for well-written legislation to make a positive difference in women's lives. Miriam Isabel Benitez, an Argentine representative for the Social Progress Party, told a member of the Latin American and Caribbean Committee for the Defense of Women's Rights, "In the course of my work I have observed that, no matter the limitations, legislation has created possibilities for the women of the region" (Benitez quoted in Miguez 2009, 6). Procedurally, "legislative modifications, especially in punitive terms" result in increases in "claims, inclusiveness in judicial information systems, and recognition that violent acts are violations of human rights" (7).

We begin this chapter by reviewing major international treaties that establish important norms and binding legal obligations regarding government's responsibility to address violence against women. Then we discuss theories of the processes by which international human rights laws and institutions affect germane legislation and respect at the local level. This is followed by a number of critiques, particularly from feminist legal scholars, hypothesizing that one shouldn't look to international law, as it is, for relief from gender-based violence. We close with a survey of empirical studies examining whether a country's treaty status matters at all with regards to whether a country honors its international legal human rights obligations.

What International Norms Are Relevant to Ending Violence against Women?

A great deal of international law provides a basis for the potential proliferation of antidiscriminatory norms and the subsequent creation of gender-violence-related domestic legislation. In a study of law and women's rights in Africa, Banda (2005) lists nearly fifty relevant international instruments, and the list would have been even longer had her study looked at all regions in the detail with which it examined Africa.

The modern (post-WWII) human rights regime that serves as the source of diffusible human rights norms began with the United Nations General Assembly's 1948 passage of the Universal Declaration of Human Rights (UDHR).

As a simple resolution, the UDHR was not legally binding on countries, but it expressed a particular vision of human dignity through its articulation of a number of inalienable, universal human rights. Included among these were the rights to not be discriminated against because of one's sex (Article 2); to life, liberty, and security of person (Article 3); to not be subjected to torture or to cruel, inhuman, or degrading treatment or punishment (Article 5); to equality before, and equal protection by, the law (Article 7); and to an effective remedy by the competent national tribunals for acts violating the fundamental rights granted by the constitution or by law (Article 8). The UDHR itself has come to be widely considered as part of customary international law (von Bernstorff 2008, 913). At minimum, it is "a serious document with enormous legal repercussions" (916).

In 1966 the International Covenant on Civil and Political Rights (ICCPR) and the International Covenant on Economic, Social, and Cultural Rights (ICESCR) gave legally binding status to the rights set forth in the UDHR. Regional treaties also came into existence, setting standards of human dignity–related behavior for states in their respective areas. These included the 1953 European Convention on Human Rights (ECHR), the 1969 American Convention on Human Rights (ACHR), and the 1981 African Charter on Human and Peoples' Rights (ACHPR). These regional treaties now also have associated courts dedicated to hearing cases. Subregional charters such as the 1994 Arab Charter on Human Rights and the Southern African Development Community's 1997 Gender Development Declaration and 1998 Addendum on Violence are also part of the tapestry of international norms relating to gender-based violence.[1]

The most important international legal instrument specifically addressing women as a particular group at risk is the Convention on the Elimination of All Forms of Discrimination against Women (CEDAW 1979). The Office of the United Nations High Commissioner for Human Rights describes the treaty as

> bringing the female half of humanity into the focus of human rights concerns. The spirit of the Convention is rooted in the goals of the United Nations: to reaffirm faith in fundamental human rights, in the dignity, and worth of the human person, in the equal rights of men and women. The present document spells out the meaning of equality and how it can be achieved. In so doing, the Convention establishes not only an international bill of rights for women, but also an agenda for action by countries to guarantee the enjoyment of those rights.[2]

The CEDAW framework included establishing the Committee on the Elimination of Discrimination against Women. This rotating body of twenty-three experts is charged with interpreting the meaning of the treaty and reviewing self-submitted quadrennial compliance reports from parties to the treaty. The committee has figured prominently in discussions regarding violence against women, as CEDAW's original text neither explicitly nor implicitly included VAW as a form of discrimination as understood by the treaty. It was not until 1992 that violence against women was explicitly incorporated into the CEDAW framework by the Committee on the Elimination of Discrimination against Women. In General Recommendation 19, the committee stated, "The definition of discrimination [in Article 1 of CEDAW] includes gender-based violence, that is, violence that is directed against a woman because she is a woman or that affects women disproportionately" (CEDAW 1992). The Committee found a basis for its finding in ten of CEDAW's sixteen substantive articles, so the incorporation of gender-based violence was substantial in both scope and depth.

In 1993 the UN General Assembly publicly strengthened its commitment to the principle of reducing violence against women via passage of its resolution, the *UN Declaration on the Elimination of Violence against Women* (DEVAW), though this was not legally binding. Additionally, the 1995 Beijing Platform for Action included violence against women as one of twelve critical areas of concern to women's dignity. Finally, in March 2011 the UN General Assembly passed Resolution 65/228, "Strengthening Crime Prevention and Criminal Justice Responses to Violence Against Women." This resolution made clear not only the General Assembly's commitment to VAW as an issue of great international concern but, in points five through ten, specifically pointed to domestic law as a critical area in reducing gender-based violence. Point nine urges member states to

> evaluate and review their legislation and legal principles, procedures, policies, programmes and practices relating to crime prevention and criminal justice matters, in a manner consistent with their legal systems and drawing upon the updated Model strategies and Practical Measures, to determine if they are adequate to prevent and eliminate violence against women. (United Nations General Assembly 2011, 4)

How Might International Law Influence the Creation of Domestic Legislation?

There are a number of different ways whereby international law might influence a state to create new legal parameters for its human rights–related behaviors, and here we survey several of these possibilities. As stated earlier, we would expect international norms both to preface domestic legal guarantees against gender-based violence in those countries without them, and to lead to improvements in legal protections in countries that already have some level of legal guarantees. Further, we would expect the recourse to law offered by domestic legal prohibitions of VAW to change societal norms about gender-based violence, however slowly, and in turn result in reduced levels of violence against women.

International-Norm-Setting

Women have the ability to help create the international laws and norms that we argue diffuse and affect the creation of domestic guarantees against gender-based violence. Hawkesworth (2012) makes a strong case that, by aiding the interpretation of treaty and statute, women's groups affect understandings and procedures relating to the function of both international and domestic institutions. For example, to have violence against women classified as a "grave breach" of Article 27 of the 1949 Geneva Convention, the Women's Caucus for Gender Justice in the International Criminal Court "began attending ICC negotiations, providing technical information about defects in existing laws, advocating changes in legal terminology, and mobilizing support for core principles of gender justice" (268). Their work resulted in an International Criminal Court with a "feminist definition of rape," equitable rules of evidence, independence from "manipulation from the UN Security Council," and improved gender equity on the court itself as compared to the International Court of Justice (269). As a result,

> In countries that ratify the Rome Statute [the treaty creating the International Criminal Court], the gender provisions could help strengthen the capacity to address violence against women at the national level via the inclusion of additional crimes of sexual and gender violence, progressive definitions of existing crimes, and more gender-sensitive procedures for the trial of these crimes. (Spees 2003, 1246)

International norms also may spread through policy diffusion (Berry and Berry 1999), which often takes place regionally as states observe the policy of others with similar political environments. Htun and Weldon (2012, 558) find that policy diffusion tends to take place among states in the same region, through "elite learning and emulation of other nations and through connections in civil society." Women's movements in one country often follow the example of successful ones in other countries (Boushey 2010). Further, research shows that nongovernmental organizations (NGOs) often work together across borders, through the sharing of ideas and resources as well as the generation of pressure (Bell et al. 2013).

Ratification and Simple Mandate

In her comprehensive study of the effect of international law on respect for human rights, Simmons (2009, 144) asserts that the mere act of a state ratifying a treaty can help move norms from the international level to the domestic level. In the immediate sense, she notes that "[a] ratified treaty *precommits* [a] government to be receptive to rights demands,"[3] as it is a "process of domestic legitimation that some scholars have shown raises the domestic salience of an international rule." Such a precommitment, via ratification, "makes it harder for a government that has secured domestic ratification to plausibly deny the importance of rights protection in the local context" (145). Simmons and Hopkins (2005, 624) add that these ratification coalitions make a ratification "more costly *ex ante* than a mere policy announcement" because such coalitions consist not only of those who desire ratification, but also of those committed to tying "the government's hands through altering the legal (and normative) setting in which policy is carved out." In the longer term, ratification can also increase the size of pro–human rights social movements through the addition of "out-of-movement supporters" (Simmons gives the example of white students joining the US civil rights movement in the 1960s) and the coalescence of broader coalitions of groups under the fabric of a ratified treaty's principles (Simmons 2009, 145–146).

Once an international treaty is ratified or its norms become part of customary international law, perhaps the simplest path toward incorporation of its norms into a domestic legal code comes via the viewpoint of "monism," which asserts that international law and domestic law are to be viewed as constituting a single body of law. The plainest assertion of monism can be found in the United States Supreme Court's decision in *The Paquete Habana* 175 U.S. 677 (1900). In that case, the court famously and bluntly stated that "international law is part of our law." Aust (2000, 146) presents three commonalities among the variations in monism: (1) "although the constitution requires the treaty to have first been approved by parliament, there are exceptions for certain types of treaties or certain circumstances"; (2) "a distinction is made between treaties according to their nature or subject matter, some being regarded as self-executing, others requiring legislation before they can have full effect in international law"; and (3) "a self-executing treaty may constitute supreme law and override any inconsistent domestic legislation." Rigaux (1998, 332) asserts that the protection of human rights is actually the best example of legal philosopher Hans Kelsen's famous position that there is no distinction between public law (relations between citizens and state), private law (relations between citizens), and international law (relations between states). Slaughter (1995, 533) points out that monism can be seen in "international 'override' provisions in domestic constitutions that mandate the supremacy of international over domestic law."

Treaty ratification could also lead to domestic legal enshrinement of international norms if a treaty were to simply require that parties create domestic law to establish the principles of that treaty. This assumes, of course, that states would do as asked, but that particular matter is an empirical question for later on in our study. Indeed, many of the major international human rights instruments contain language directing domestic law to be brought into conformity with the guarantees of those international norms. The CEDAW states that parties must "incorporate the principle of equality of men and women in their legal system, abolish all discriminatory laws and adopt appropriate ones prohibiting discrimination against women." Article 2(2) of the ICCPR requires that "where not already provided for by existing legislative or other measures, each State Party to the present Covenant undertakes to take the necessary steps . . . to adopt such laws or other measures as may be necessary to give effect to the rights recognized in the present Covenant." However, no such mandate exists for those rights guaranteed by the ICESCR. These mandates clearly demonstrate that the founders of these treaties believed firmly that ensuring human dignity necessitates the enshrinement of international principles in domestic legal codes. The lack of such a mandate in the ICESCR adds credence to that idea, as it was a particularly difficult treaty to found and many major powers, such as the United States, would have been keen to weaken it as much as possible. One way to weaken a treaty is via the absence of mandated domestic legal enshrinement of its principles by states' parties.

Like the ICCPR, Article 2 of the ACHR and Article 1 of the ACHPR require domestic law to be used to bring a state into conformity with the treaty's guarantees whenever necessary. The ECHR carries no direct mandate for domestic institution of its guarantees, but Article 57 is an implicit nod to the importance of domestic legal enshrinement: "On receipt of a request from the Secretary-General of the Council of Europe any High Contracting Party shall furnish an explanation of the manner in which its internal law ensures the effective implementation of any of the provisions of this Convention." In this way, the ECHR sends a strong message about the role of domestic law in enshrining these principles.

Both Landman (2005) and Simmons (2009) find empirical evidence that treaty ratification is reliably associated with greater levels of respect for human rights. Both studies contain important asterisks, however. Landman finds that whether a state lives up to any particular human rights treaty's obligation is conditional upon the strength of the state's reservations to that treaty. Simmons is persuaded that governments ratify treaties because they intend to comply with them. The asterisk here is that "governments ratify when their preferences line up with the contents of the treaty." For example, "democratic governments were the most likely to ratify treaties that replicate the kinds of rights they already tend to have in place" (108–109), whereas nondemocratic governments tend not to ratify treaties that would obligate them to provide civil and political rights to individuals. These findings sharply contradict those of earlier studies showing either no ratification effects on behavior or that ratification represents an empty promise easily made by the most repressive states (Hafner-Burton and Tsutsui 2007; Hathaway 2002; Keith 1999).

Given that the most important and common factor in seemingly all empirical studies of treaty commitment is regime type, it is unclear whether treaty obligations to an instrument such as CEDAW would bear substantively on a state's incorporation of anti-VAW principles into its domestic code. This is because violence against women is a pandemic—unlike such notorious human rights violations as political imprisonment, torture, and the denial of freedom of movement. However, Simmons's (2009, 202–255) findings suggest that by greater access to independent courts and with greater opportunity for social mobilization, democracy might affect the ability to translate international norms into domestic legal protections against gender-based violence.

Advocacy Networks

Another possible method of diffusion comes from Risse and Sikkink (1999, 5), who advance an argument also made by Keck and Sikkink (1998) that the diffusion of international human rights norms to the domestic level happens via the work of advocacy networks that "constitute necessary conditions for sustainable domestic change." Keck and Sikkink's theory, known popularly as the boomerang model, posits that activist groups in a country pressure external actors for help in realizing human rights, thereby setting into effect a boomerang of pressure from external actors onto the government of the citizens who made the initial appeal. The processes by which these transnational networks affect human rights attitudes and policies at the local level include "put[ting] norm-violating states on the international agenda in terms of moral consciousness-raising," "empower[ing] and legitimat[ing] the claims of domestic opposition groups against norm-violating governments," and "challeng[ing] norm-violating governments by creating a transnational structure pressuring such regimes simultaneously 'from above' and 'from below'" (Risse and Sikkink 1999, 5).

Aside from the many case studies demonstrating the effectiveness of social mobilization on political outcomes, there are now emerging large-scale comparative analyses showing the effects of domestic social mobilizations upon treaty ratification and human rights–related outcomes. For example, Kang (2011) examines forty-seven African countries from 2000 through 2011 and finds action by women's social mobilization groups to be reliably associated with both increased state ratification of the Maputo Protocol on the Rights of Women in Africa (1995) and the domestic adoption of gender quotas. Neuemayer (2005, 950) found that for human rights-treaty ratification to be translated into actual respect for human rights, there must exist "conditions for domestic groups, parties, and individuals and for civil society" to convince or cajole government to do so. He concluded that where civil-society groups are absent, ratification of a human rights treaty can make affairs worse than they would have been otherwise.

It is one thing to diffuse norms or affect government behavior in a particular case, and another to incorporate these norms into domestic law. In legal scholarship, the process by which international norms are internalized into domestic law is called transnational legal process. Koh (2007, 567) argues that any number of types of actors—"transnational norm entrepreneurs, governmental norm sponsors, transnational issue networks, and interpretive communities"—can play a role in this process: "One of these agents triggers an interaction at the international level, works together with other agents of internalization to force an interpretation of the international legal norm in an interpretive forum, and then continues to work with these agents to persuade a resisting nation-state to internalize that interpretation into domestic law" (ibid.). This is akin to Keck and Sikkink's boomerang model; in both models international actors affect local norms. However, in Koh's formulation of transnational legal process, the impetus for norm domestication does not necessarily always come "from the bottom" (from in-country groups). Further, this process is iterative, meaning that it is through repeated cycles of "interaction-interpretation-internalization" that international norms become part of a domestic legal system (568).

International Rulings

Rulings by international bodies could affect domestic legal systems with regards to VAW. By establishing authoritative interpretations of states' duties and behaviors with regard to international norms, these rulings could establish frames of interpretation and recourse around which local actors could organize. These frames could include the necessity of establishing domestic legal guarantees. For example, the importance of the adoption of full and explicit domestic legal guarantees protecting women from violence was clearly demonstrated in a groundbreaking July 2011 decision by the Inter-American Commission on Human Rights (IACHR). In *Lenahan (Gonzales) v. United States*,[4] the commission ruled that the United States needed to do more to protect victims of domestic violence.

In 1999 Jessica (Lenahan) called on police in Castle Rock, Colorado, to enforce a restraining order against her estranged husband, who had taken her three daughters. The police did not enforce the restraining order, and the three girls were murdered by the estranged husband. Gonzales's case reached the United States Supreme Court, which decided 7–2 that Castle Rock and its local police could not be sued for failing to enforce a restraining order, as "for Due Process Clause purposes, [Gonzales did not have] a property interest in police enforcement of the restraining order against her husband" (*Castle Rock v. Gonzales*).[5] That is, she had no federal right to sue. The response of the American Civil Liberties Union, which organized nine friend-of-the-court briefs, was telling in its call for better domestic legislation. Lenora Lapidus, director of the ACLU Women's Rights Project, said that "the Supreme Court's ruling makes it clear that state legislatures must take the lead in protecting victims of domestic violence and pass laws that will hold police accountable for taking protection orders seriously" (ACLU 2005).

Gonzales's lawyers then appealed to the IACHR on her behalf, citing that the United States violated Articles 1 (the right to life, liberty, and personal security), 2 (right to equality before the law), 5 (right to protection of honor, personal reputation, and private and family life), 6 (right to a family and to protection thereof), 7 (right to protection for mothers and children), 9 (right to inviolability of the home), 18 (right to a fair trial), and 24 (right of petition) of the American Declaration of the Rights and Duties of Man (1948) by "failing to exercise due diligence to protect Jessica Lenahan and her daughters from acts of domestic violence perpetrated by the ex-husband of the former and the father of the latter" (Organization of American States 2011, 1).[6] The position of the United States in the matter was that Colorado had a mandatory-arrest law in place, but in phone conversations with police, Gonzalez never characterized the restraining order as having been broken or the presence of the three girls with their father as constituting abduction. Further, the United States claimed,

> The petitioners cite no provision of the American Declaration that imposes on the United States an affirmative duty, such as the exercise of due diligence, to prevent the commission of individual crimes by private parties . . . [and as a] legal matter, the United States maintains that it is not bound by obligations contained in human rights treaties it has not joined and the substantive obligations enshrined in these instruments cannot be imported into the American Declaration. (Organization of American States 2011, 12)

The latter half of this response is of particular interest, as the United States makes the case it is not explicitly bound by customary international law. First, custom is well and long understood as one of the primary sources of international law. Second, what are the implications of such a stance? The United States did not sign the 1948 international genocide convention until 1988. However, the ban on genocide had long been considered *jus cogens*—a peremptory norm of international law—binding on all states, without any exception. Had the United States not considered itself bound by this norm from 1948 through 1988?

The commission stated that it had "repeatedly interpreted the American Declaration as requiring States to adopt measures to give legal effect to the rights contained in the American Declaration" (33), and that not only is gender-based violence "one of the most extreme and pervasive forms of discrimination" but "various international human rights bodies have moreover considered State failures in the realm of domestic violence not only discriminatory, but also violations to the right to life of women" (30). Thus, "all States have a legal obligation to protect women from domestic violence," as this is "a problem widely recognized by the international community as a serious human rights violation and an extreme form of discrimination" (Organization of American States 2011, 44). Furthermore, states have a "legal obligation to respect and ensure the right not to discriminate and to equal protection of the law [and this] due diligence obligation in principle applies to all OAS Member States" (ibid.).

In a 2007 report titled "Access to Justice for Women Victims of Violence in the Americas," the commission identified "the duty of State parties to adopt legal measures to prevent imminent acts of violence . . . and identified restraining orders, and their adequate and effective enforcement, among these legal measures" (Organization of American States 2007, 47). However, bad laws can be worse than no laws at all. The report bemoans the state of civil and criminal laws in place in American states:

> Outdated laws remain in force, as do discriminatory provisions based on ste-reotypes of the role of women in society . . . Some countries still have laws that grant a rapist relief from punishment if he agrees to marry his victim . . . even today the law focuses basically on domestic and intrafamily violence, to the exclusion of other forms of violence perpetrated against women . . . outside of and apart from home and family. (Organization of American States ibid., xi)

A rape victim being forced to marry her attacker is a likely road to what is called, among other things, "secondary victimization." Victims of violence who are treated insensitively (or worse) by authorities, family, and/or society can experi-ence magnified feelings of "powerlessness, shame, and guilt" Campbell (1998, 356). These negative feelings can be powerful—akin to experiencing a "second rape" (Campbell and Raja 1999).

Moreover, the commission found that a state can indeed be responsible for the actions of nonstate actors. It cited the 2005 case of the Mapiripán Massacre, in which the Inter-American Court of Human Rights found states to have a positive obligation to adopt the measures necessary to ensure effective protection of human rights in interpersonal relationships (Organization of American States 2007). These duties of protection, the commission found, were not fulfilled by the United States in the case of Jessica Gonzales.

What are the odds of a state incorporating the substance of international rulings into domestic legislation? Hawkins and Jacoby (2010) find that states often partially comply with international court judgments and are relatively less likely to comply with reparations orders concerning the adoption, amendment, or repeal of domestic legislation. However, recent work argues that international courts' legal rulings often have influence beyond the states involved in particular cases. For example, Helfer and Voeten (2014) find that European Court of Hu-man Rights judgments against one country greatly increase the probability of domestic-policy change across Europe. Hillebrecht (2012, 985) reminds us that, when answering this question, one must not forget that such incorporation is the result of a decidedly political process, varying from state to state. Executives, in particular, serve as "gatekeepers" of compliance. For example,

> When an executive has sufficient political will for compliance, as well as institu-tional support from judges and legislators, as in Argentina, compliance with the

Inter-American tribunals' rulings and recommendations can have a powerful effect on human rights . . . [whereas] power imbalance and competing demands on the executive can grind compliance to a halt, as in Colombia.

The Enlargement Approach

The process of formal incorporation of international law into a country's domestic legal code can be a tricky and contentious business, even when important political actors are willing. Yet there is a way domestic legal entities can almost unilaterally incorporate international norms into domestic legal systems. Since international law is seldom explicitly self-executing, many courts wishing to heed international standards will interpret an existing domestic statute or constitutional provision in relation to its complementarity with the country's international obligations. We call this the enlargement approach. For example, the Botswana Court of Appeal wrote in *Attorney General v. Unity Dow.*[7]

> We should so far as is possible so interpret domestic legislation so as not to conflict with Botswana's obligations under the [African Charter on Human Rights] or other international obligations. . . . Unless . . . it is impossible to do otherwise, it would be wrong for its Courts to interpret its legislation in a manner which conflicts with the international obligations Botswana has undertaken. (Ross 2008, 388–389)

In *Vishaka v. Rajasthan,*[8] the Supreme Court of India considered how to provide protection to women in the workplace in the absence of domestic legal protections. Similar to the case in Botswana, the court decided,

> In the absence of domestic law occupying the field, to formulate effective measures to check the evil of sexual harassment of working women . . . the contents of the International Conventions and norms are significant for the purpose of the interpretation of [the Indian Constitution's] guarantee of gender equality, [and] the right to work with human dignity. . . . Any international convention not inconsistent with the fundamental rights and in harmony with [the Indian Constitution's] spirit must be read into the provisions to enlarge the meaning and content. (Ross 2008, 395)

While it is gratifying to have judges use international law to expand the meaning of domestic codes and/or constitutions in the absence of explicit domestic legal guarantees, this is not a position of strength for those wishing to reduce gender-based discrimination. The weakness is due to the fact that the enlargement approach depends entirely on the preferences of individual jurists. A monist and a dualist would probably react quite differently to a similar gender-violence-based case, with the latter most likely to skip enlarging domestic meanings via international law. The inherent weakness of the enlargement approach is one reason for our argument in this book that the strongest legal arrangement for reducing gender-based violence is to have explicit domestic legal guarantees to which judges must be accountable without having to rely on individual discretion to explicitly reach toward international law to protect women from violence.

Internalization

Internalization is "the acceptance of a norm by actors within [an] organization who are persuaded of its merits and validity through such processes as social learning, framing, and deliberation" (Sarfaty 2009, 649). Merry (2003, 943) describes how international human rights law relating to gender discrimination can help internalize the understandings contained in this law by "alter[ing] the meanings of gender and of state responsibility for gender equality." One way this is accomplished is by mandating that factors like tradition and religion not be allowed to excuse infractions of law to which countries have become party. Merry notes that DEVAW (1993) requires countries "to condemn violence against women and not to invoke custom, religion, or culture to limit their obligations" (946). Creating legal frameworks to modify behavior, such as those that would prevent custom, religion, or culture from preventing the domestic institution of international norms, is a form of coercion.

Scholars of legal semiotics point out that human rights can be seen as both a package and something to be packaged, "not simply a legal creation but an extraordinary feat of political imagination" (Gies 2011, 420). Human rights offer a universal connection via "a symbolic framework for the bonds which make us human" (421). Acculturation results when "groups of individuals having different cultures come into continuous first-hand contact, with subsequent changes in the original culture patterns of either or both groups" (Berry 2008, 330). While most often applied to study the relationships between migrant and host populations, the lens of acculturation can also be applied to the phenomenon of an international norm being globalized through international law and affecting a "host" country that is party to some treaty. Goodman and Jinks (2008, 727) make the case that, with regard to the internalization of human rights law, "many instances of acculturation include complete internalization of global scripts." Sometimes acculturation toward human rights acceptance can be led by a charismatic individual such as Nelson Mandela (South Africa), Václav Havel (Czech Republic), and Kim Dae Jung (South Korea) (Koh 2005, 981). However, not all internalization need be earnest. Internalization via acculturation may "entail the adoption of norms without belief in their content" (Goodman and Jinks 2004; Sarfaty 2009, 649).

The Counterargument: International Law May Be of No Help

Even with the existence of much gender-violence-related international law and with many NGOs seeking outside assistance via framing violations of human dignity using international norms, international law may not, ultimately, affect domestic legislation. In this section, we survey several sources of skepticism about international law's ability to effect positive change on gender-based violence by means of domestic legislation.

Whose Boomerang?

While simple in theory, the boomerang model of international human rights norms diffusing via advocacy networks has many complexities and challenges. First, Santos (2005) cautions that this process must be viewed as a double-edged sword. While conferences such as the 1993 United Nations Conference on Human Rights in Vienna allowed feminists to collectively engage the international policy process, such activities also distance NGO professionals from "local feminist mobilizations" (60). Second, Bob (2005, 5) argues that countries typically have many competing interests looking for the boost of the boomerang as "competition for NGO intervention occurs in a context of economic, political, and organizational inequality that systematically advantages some challengers over others." Thus it is possible that in an environment of varied interests competing for external attention, voices seeking to be heard on the topic of violence against women may not be heard. According to Bob's argument, this would likely be because other groups were more media savvy and resource laden.

Third, Hertel (2006a and 2006b) offers a nuanced accounting of differences within the groups petitioning for assistance, and argues that the ways these intragroup differences are processed are an important factor in how local understandings of international norms evolve. This is different from Bob's competition-based hypothesis, wherein one interest might actively block another's success. Hertel gives the example of Bangladeshi activists being divided on the issue of child labor in textile plants. There were two camps in opposition, both from a rights-based perspective: those supporting a proposed US bill that would have levied sanctions against countries with child labor in export industries, and those who argued that the bill would have driven 40,000 to 50,000 children out of work from an industry responsible for 74 percent of Bangladesh's exports (Hertel 2006a, 267). The first group made an argument based on the 1959 UN Declaration on the Rights of the Child and an International Labor Organization rule on minimum working age. At the same time, Bangladeshi groups opposing this bill made a human rights argument on the grounds of "physical integrity rights," claiming that the newly unemployed children would, by and large, fall into lives of prostitution (268–269). Hertel concludes,

> Many Bangladeshi activists insist that while the elimination of child labor may be desirable in the long run, the reality of children's need to work under nonexploitive conditions must be balanced with the right to a decent standard of living and the right to education. Blocking brought such normative distinctions to the fore in this campaign—and fueled a debate over children's rights that moved well beyond the campaign itself. (270)

Fourth, while Weldon (2002) agrees that "women's movements are a *necessary* condition for the initial articulation" (195)[9] of the issue of gender-based violence, she is careful to point out that despite these social movements' ability to facilitate norm diffusion—even to the point of treaty ratification—public policy is typically made within male-dominated structures. Therefore, without an effective "women's policy machinery" (126, 154) to competently turn issues into action (legislation), social movements can go only so far in translating international gender-equity norms into enforceable public policy. Weldon casts these policy machineries as facilitating relationships between outsiders (those appealing from without the public-policy-making system for reforms) and insiders (those who work within the public-policy-making system). Her empirical investigation of thirty-six "stable democracies" showed that "where there is no effective women's policy machinery, the insider-outsider partnerships tend to produce partial, fragmented responses; [but] where there is such an agency, the partnerships are more likely to result in broad, multifaceted policies to address violence against women" (196). Building an effective women's policy machinery can be a difficult, even dangerous task, as evidenced by the July 2012 car-bomb assassination of, Hanifa Safi, head of women's affairs in the eastern Laghman Province of Afghanistan.

Finally, the successful and complete diffusion of international norms into legally binding local codes may be an imperfectly cumulative process, however it is initiated. Hevener (1986) outlined the incorporation of women's rights–based norms into domestic laws, via norms contained in international law, as a three-step sequence. The first step is the existence of "protective provisions," where "women are usually treated as subordinates when outside their traditional domestic sphere" and "laws and legal practices . . . codify an implied rather than a defined inferiority" so that women remain in a subordinate role to men (72). Hevener notes it is in this way that women are likened to children: wards of the patriarchal state, needing rational decisions made on their behalf (as women are unable to do so themselves). An example of this would be the following statement made in 1969 by Rhodesia's minister of internal affairs in explanation for the rejection of a proposal that would have granted legal personhood to women for the first time since independence:[10] "The present position is that ninety nine percent of African women would find legal emancipation of that nature quite intolerable. It would be disastrous to do anything too quickly" (Banda 2005, 13–14).

The second step is "corrective provisions," which "contain the implication that in some particular area women are not being treated fairly and that an effort to improve their treatment in that specific area is needed" (Hevener 1986, 74). These provisions are typically targeted at some very specific area, such as sex trafficking or a woman's right to a nationality (74–75).

The third and final step is the institution of "non-discriminatory provisions," which seek to "revise the legal system in such a way that gender will no longer be a basis for the allocation of benefits and burdens in society" (78). Hevener cautions, however, that there is nothing in nondiscriminatory provisions maintaining that "(a) there are no differences whatever between the sexes, (b) such differences ought to be eliminated, or (c) cultural characteristics presently associated with the female sex should be eliminated from the society" (78).

Reservations

The question of what states are parties to what treaties seems, on its face, a simple one: states that have signed and ratified (or acceded to) a treaty are parties to it. The question of what rules a state party to a treaty has agreed to follow also seems straightforward—those rules written in the body of the treaty. Not so fast, however. In both cases, states can make reservations to treaties to which they choose to become a party. When issuing a reservation, a country states what parts of the treaty it disavows (whole articles and/or specific paragraphs) and why. By doing so, states make their support conditional rather than unqualified.

It may seem counterintuitive to allow states to make their support for a treaty conditional, but by doing so and avoiding an all-or-nothing approach, the likelihood of broader involvement in a treaty increases. Additionally, there are limits on what types of reservations a state may make and still be considered a party to a treaty. The 1969 Vienna Convention on the Law of Treaties states in Article 19(c) that a country may, "when signing, ratifying, accepting, approving or acceding to a treaty, formulate a reservation unless . . . the reservation is incompatible with the *object and purpose* of the treaty."[11] That is, a state's reservations to a treaty cannot render the treaty essentially useless.

Which states make the most reservations? Neumayer (2007) finds that liberal democracies make more reservations than do other types of states. This is due to the fact, he argues, that liberal democracies take their treaty obligations seriously, but "like any other nation-state, want to limit the extent of interference with their sovereignty" (401). Landman (2005, 7) shows, however, that states that became democratic in the 1990–1994 "fourth wave" are less likely to make reservations than are states with longer tenures as democracies.

Reservations come in different forms and strengths. Some are based on very narrow technical issues with treaty language and do not end up affecting a state's commitment to the principal objective of the treaty. For instance, China's reservation to CEDAW reads, "The People's Republic of China does not consider itself bound by paragraph 1 of Article 29 of the Convention." Indeed, great number of states submitted a reservation regarding Article 29(1). However, this reservation is not seen as incompatible with CEDAW's object and purpose. Article 29(1) reads,

> Any dispute between two or more States Parties concerning the interpretation or application of the present Convention which is not settled by negotiation shall, at the request of one of them, be submitted to arbitration. If within six months from the date of the request for arbitration the parties are unable to agree on the organization of the arbitration, any one of those parties may refer the dispute to the International Court of Justice by request in conformity with the Statute of the Court.

On the other hand, more substantive types of reservations might put a state in a situation whereby a reservation eliminates a state's obligation toward a vital part of the treaty. Article 2 of CEDAW states,

> States Parties condemn discrimination against women in all its forms, agree to pursue by all appropriate means and without delay a policy of eliminating discrimination against women and, to this end, undertake:
>
> (a) To embody the principle of the equality of men and women in their national constitutions or other appropriate legislation if not yet incorporated therein and to ensure, through law and other appropriate means, the practical realization of this principle;
>
> (b) To adopt appropriate legislative and other measures, including sanctions where appropriate, prohibiting all discrimination against women;
>
> (c) To establish legal protection of the rights of women on an equal basis with men and to ensure through competent national tribunals and other public institutions the effective protection of women against any act of discrimination;
>
> (d) To refrain from engaging in any act or practice of discrimination against women and to ensure that public authorities and institutions shall act in conformity with this obligation;
>
> (e) To take all appropriate measures to eliminate discrimination against women by any person, organization or enterprise;
>
> (f) To take all appropriate measures, including legislation, to modify or abolish existing laws, regulations, customs and practices which constitute discrimination against women;
>
> (g) To repeal all national penal provisions which constitute discrimination against women.

The Committee on the Elimination of Discrimination against Women regards Article 2 to be a "core provision" of CEDAW and maintains that reserving an obligation to respect this article amounts to an impermissible reservation (CEDAW 2012). Nonetheless, nine state parties to CEDAW have made reservations against the entirety of Article 2: Algeria, Bahrain, Bangladesh, Egypt, Lesotho, Libya, Morocco, Singapore, and Syria. For example, Bahrain makes its reservation to Article 2 "in order to ensure its implementation within the bounds of the provisions of the Islamic Shariah," while "the Government of the People's Republic of Bangladesh does not consider as binding upon itself the provisions of Article 2, . . . as they conflict with Sharia law based on Holy Quran and Sunna." In total, sixteen state parties make an objection to at least some part of Article 2, as seven other states make a partial reservation against:

2(a): Bahamas
2(d): Niger
2(f): Niger, Iraq, Federated States of Micronesia, United Arab Emirates, Democratic People's Republic of Korea, New Zealand
2(g): Iraq

Certainly, not all countries that are party to the treaty agree with these reservations and they can make their objections known in writing. For example,

> The Government of Denmark considers that the reservations made by the United Arab Emirates to article 2 (f), 15 (2) and 16 referring to the contents of the Shariah Law do not clearly specify the extent to which the United Arab Emirates feel committed to the object and purpose of the Convention. Consequently, the Government of Denmark considers the said reservations as being incompatible with the object and purpose of the Convention and accordingly inadmissible and without effect under international law.

How researchers treat the issues of reservation legitimacy and party status will affect their findings. We explicitly incorporate states' CEDAW reservations in the forthcoming empirical analyses. And while many reservations to CEDAW are of interest when one is examining laws addressing violence against women, the countries that have made reservations against Article 2 will be of particular interest, as this article explicitly frames the importance of national legislation in efforts to reduce gender-based violence.

Feminist Critiques

Some feminist scholarship is doubtful or even dismissive of the idea that international law has anything to offer toward the improvement of women's lives. Some also critique a focus on violence against women itself as being "gender-essentialist." The debates among feminists on treating women as a group, the role of law in affecting women's lives, and women's rights as human rights, among other matters, are longstanding and theoretically rich. While it's beyond the scope of this book to directly address these debates with any theoretical substance, they unquestionably bring important and relevant critiques to bear on our study. In this section, we highlight a few key arguments.

Since feminism, largely, regards international and other forms of law as making claims to inherent objectivity and universality, feminist legal methods "seek to expose and question the limited bases of . . . law's claim [to objectivity and universality]" (Charlesworth 1999, 379).[12] That is, while "traditional legal methods place a high premium on the predictability, certainty, and fixity of rules," feminist legal methods "emerged from the critique that existing rules overrepresent existing power structures" and instead value "rule-flexibility and the ability to identify missing points of view" (Bartlett 1990, 832). Typically, these "missing" views come from women and minorities.

Whose worldview, then, forms the basis for law? Feminists see government and law as gendered entities, meaning they have been created and dominated by male views. Charlesworth and Chinkin (1993, 67) posit that "even with something as sacred as *jus cogens*—the category of peremptory [authoritatively inviolable] norms of international law—masculine thinking prevails." For example, in the established violations of *jus cogens* (e.g., slavery, genocide, murder, torture, and systematic racial discrimination) they see little or no evidence of the types of violations informed by women's experience. Former International Court of Justice judge Bruno Simma and former United Nations Special Rapporteur Philip Alston reinforce that this is a problem, adding that any human rights legal theories addressing race to the exclusion of gender discrimination are "flawed in terms [of] both . . . theory of human rights and of United Nations doctrine" (68).

So, some real change in law's content would be necessary for it to give proper address to issues of particular concern to women, nonetheless to VAW. Doing so may be structurally difficult. Law is created by those with the political power to use political institutions for their purposes—however noble or ignoble. When feminists label government as a gendered entity, they mean males have historically dominated political, social, and economic power. To the extent that is true, alternative worldviews (such as those of women) are not represented in law. This provides a quite uneven playing field in the competition over law's content and meaning. Brown notes that women are unequal participants in the social contract upon which popular governance rests, as a contract "presumes individuals abstracted from relations of power or equal within those relations" (1995, 162). Further, women's use of law for their own ends assumes some legal literacy, and that can be very difficult given the challenge of adequate dissemination of legal information to women (Tsanga 2007). In many countries women have less access to formal education than do men; where this is true, a woman's ability to read and comprehend disseminated materials may be stunted.

Further, what exactly does it mean to say something has been done "with women in mind" or from a "woman's perspective"? Is it even possible to say something is done from a "woman's perspective"? Would the claim of objectivity seen by feminists as inherent in law be more acceptable if that same objectivity incorporated the views of women such that they might affect their own legal destiny? Not necessarily.

On one hand, it seems plausible that women being abused at the hands of intimate familiars, strangers, bosses, state officials, and the like would have a very different view of what legal changes are necessary—relative to violence against women—than would males who are not regularly experiencing violence at home and in public, no matter the other differences among the victims. Indeed, an adherent to standpoint feminism might say, "Yes, it is possible to talk meaningfully about a 'woman's perspective'." Standpoint feminism views women (as a group) as having an inherently different experience from that of men—each group's experience having derived from its social position (Weldon 2006, 64). Therefore, while there does exist some innate "women's perspective" it differs from its male counterpart.

On the other hand, for some this raises the specter of gender essentialism, which can be described as "overgeneralized claims about women" (Kapur 2005, 99) or "using women's experience as the source of explanation rather than as what requires analysis" (Mardorossian 2002, 745). Postmodernist feminists such as Sylvester (1994) criticize standpoint feminism for stifling alternative perspectives due to its view of all women as a group functioning as a unitary actor with a single mind and voice. Goodmark (2012, 23) calls this unitary actor view the "We the Women" position and notes that it ultimately squelches differences among women "in favor of presenting one voice." One effect of this in the early women's movement, she argues, was "to silence the voices of women of color" in favor of a female universal that was "white, straight, and socioeconomically privileged" (ibid.).

This is not to say all feminist critics see legal improvements as an impossibility. Some simply see improvement as requiring a quite complex accounting for the great variance in life experience among women. *Intersectionality* is a term for the way in which women's multiple roles and/or identities might interact with one another to create a situation where women experience human rights violations quite differently from one another. Essentialist perspectives do not account for the experience of women who "suffer discrimination based on multiple systems of oppression operating simultaneously, such as racism, classism, ethnocentrism, sexism, and heterosexism" (Bond 2003, 80). Therefore, a feminism that pays respect to the experiential variations among women may be able to provide better lives for domestic violence victims. This is because the "complexity of women's experiences of abuse" would inform a woman-centered system where "defining domestic violence around the woman's experience would allow the legal system to move away from narrowly drawn categories of abuse" and toward understanding that "myriad actions and omissions can constitute abuse" (Goodmark 2012, 139).

Also, it's worth noting that the essentialist critique is not entirely lost on the law. For example, Article 5 of the CEDAW treaty clearly links the subordination of women with stereotyped roles and states that maternity is a social function, with men and women having a common responsibility for the "upbringing and development" of their children. That is, stereotyping is discrimination. However, critics such as Kapur (2005) might counter that even Article 5 is subject to cultural essentialism in its provision of a seeming single model of parental responsibility for childrearing.

An important feminist critique of international law itself is that it stereotypes women as victims. Charlesworth (1999, 381) explains that "when women enter into focus at all in international law, they are viewed in a very limited way, often as victims, particularly as mothers, or potential mothers, in need of protection." Merry's (2006) account of the drafting of the consensual conference document following the Beijing + Five conference in 2000 provides an example of how women can get stereotyped into a particular role for the purposes of an international instrument. The issue of a woman's role in the family created a divide between the Holy See and the Group of 77 (G77) caucus of developing countries. Both entities emphasized the importance of the family, but they diverged about a woman's role in that institution. The Holy See emphasized the significance of "maternity, motherhood" and "the upbringing of the family" (41). The G77, on the other hand, emphasized that women "continue to bear disproportionate burden in the household responsibilities" and that this must be addressed through law, policies, and programs (41). Both points of view ended up in the final document.

One result of stereotyping women as mothers, family care providers, and the like is that women's policy issues—domestic violence, for example—can be separated from other, related policy issues. This makes it more difficult to forge integrated policy solutions—an important ability in complex matters such as gender-based violence—and can move woman-centric issues such as family violence off the radar of ongoing interest and/or discussion. Further, such stereotyping can mix with other possible restraints upon political-legal attempts to effectively address issues of real importance to women, in particular.

Earlier we discussed Weldon's (2002) caveat that while social movements are useful, they don't have much effect in the absence of a woman's policy machinery. The caucus of feminist negotiators taking part in the South African constitutional deliberations in the 1990s serves as a good example of this. Having studied "women's machinery" in countries around the world, these women were concerned that, constructed poorly, a "woman's ministry" could end up restricting women's issues by "limiting their scope to . . . domestic relations, child care, nutrition, health, and handicrafts" as well as separating women's issues from other issues (Hawkesworth 2012, 183). This scope of issues is grossly gender-stereotypical with its dominant focus on childcare, other private sphere-activities, and crafts. Certainly, the matter of violence against women would not be included in such an issue set. The caucus ended up establishing a Commission on Gender Equality "with the responsibility to *oversee the operations of all units of government* to ensure full implementation of the gender provisions in the constitution" (183).[13]

Conclusion

There are good reasons to believe that international law may be able to stimulate the creation of domestic statutes aimed at protecting women from sexual assault and harassment. Further, there is some anecdotal evidence that such statutes may work in providing justice for victims and may be reducing the number of VAW crimes. On the other hand, there are plausible arguments that international law is not a fruitful means to stimulate domestic legislation on gender violence. Further, law itself as an entity may be so entrenched in gendered power structures that it cannot be helpful in reducing violence against women. Finally, some feel even treating women as a group with a unique, common experience regarding certain forms of violence may be impossible or counterproductive.

Our next several chapters will introduce and use a methodology to empirically examine these wide-ranging viewpoints. Here we list the hypotheses generated by the discussions in this chapter. First come the hypotheses we test in this book and second are hypotheses that may be interesting for future research.

Hypotheses Tested in This Book

- To the extent that countries within a given region adopt domestic laws addressing gender-based violence, other countries in that region are more likely to adopt domestic laws addressing gender-based violence.
- To the extent that countries within a given region adopt stronger domestic laws addressing gender-based violence, other countries in that region are more likely to adopt *strong* domestic laws addressing gender-based violence.

- Countries that are parties to international instruments addressing violence against women are *more likely* than others to have *any* domestic legal guarantees against gender-based violence.
- Countries that are parties to international instruments addressing violence against women are *more likely* than others to have *comprehensive* domestic legal guarantees against gender-based violence.
- Countries with greater numbers of domestic and international advocate groups are *more likely* than others to have *any* domestic legal prohibitions on violence against women.
- Countries with greater numbers of domestic and international advocate groups are *more likely* than others to have *comprehensive* domestic legal prohibitions on violence against women.

Hypotheses Needing Further Research

- To the extent women's groups are involved in the creation of international norms relating to violence against women, domestic laws addressing gender-based violence should be *more prevalent* in countries around the world.
- To the extent women's groups are involved in the creation of international norms relating to violence against women, domestic laws addressing gender-based violence should be *stronger* in countries around the world.
- Countries against which an international body has ruled on a gender violence–related matter are *more likely* than others to have *any* domestic legal prohibitions on violence against women.
- Countries against which an international body has ruled on a gender violence–related matter are *more likely* than others to have *comprehensive* domestic legal prohibitions on violence against women.
- Countries whose highest courts interpret domestic statute or constitutional provisions in relation to their complementarity with their country's international obligations are more likely to have *comprehensive* domestic legal prohibitions on violence against women.
- To the extent countries disallow the invocation of custom, religion, or culture to limit their obligations to protect women from violence of all kinds, these countries are more likely to have *comprehensive* domestic legal prohibitions on violence against women.

CHAPTER 4

CREATING INDICATORS OF LEGAL GUARANTEES

In this chapter, we detail the creation of our original data on the presence and strength of four types of domestic statutes addressing violence against women (VAW). Because the quantitative approach is not common in international-relations literature addressing women's lives, we begin the chapter by briefly addressing some common concerns about this type of methodology. Next we provide an overview of existing measures of gender-violence laws, explaining why we consider our data to be an improvement necessary to address the research questions posed earlier in the book. Finally, we describe the creation of our original cross-national legal data. In doing so, we introduce readers to a simple measurement methodology that is hopefully transparent enough that it can be used to create indicators of many laws other than those addressed in this book.

A Few Words on the Quantitative and Qualitative Approaches to Scholarly Inquiry

Measurement is the foundation of quantitative scholarship, and in many of the disciplines and research programs in the social sciences, debate over the relative worth of quantitative and qualitative scholarship is ongoing. The authors' own discipline of political science has been rife with intense debate between these two traditions. Schrodt (2006, 335) characterizes the tenor of the exchanges as follows: "While this debate is not in any sense about religion, its dynamics are best understood as though it were." The stakes in the debate are high; quantitative and qualitative scholars differ in such crucial matters as approaches to explanation, conception of causation, scope and generalization, determination of which cases are considered substantively important, and concepts and measurement (Mahoney and Goertz 2006, 229). This divide in scholarly approach is evident in the literature on women's rights, status, and capability, and the debate is not purely academic. For example, Richards and Gelleny (2007) point out that the qualitative and quantitative literatures on the relationship between globalization and women's status have developed nearly uniformly different conclusions to similar research questions.

Important Measurement Terms

Concept: A concept is the thing being measured. It can be something directly observable, such as the number of one's children, or something abstract, such as democracy.

Measure: Also known as an *indicator,* a quantitative measure is a system by which the quantity and/or quality of concepts can be expressed in numeric form. The actual numeric scores produced and assigned to some entity being assessed (e.g., countries or people) are known collectively as *data.*

Validity: A measure is valid when it measures what it says it is measuring. Invalid measures are often either missing some key part of the concept being measured or contain some element unrelated to the concept being measured. For example, a measure of torture that does not include mental as well as physical torture would be lacking in validity. Likewise, a valid measure of a child's spelling ability would not include how well the child can do subtraction.

Reliability: A reliable measure is a consistent measure. One important form of reliability is known as *interrater reliability,* and that is when different persons applying the same measurement rules to the same information sources produce the same data.

Transparency: It is important that the measurement systems by which data are created are openly available for inspection. This is particularly necessary to ascertain validity. To the extent measurement schemes are transparent, resultant data should be replicable. Being able to reproduce another's data is important for establishing reliability.

What is uncontested is that the usage of quantitative data for scholarship and for evidence-based policymaking has grown over the last few decades. Sally Engle Merry (2011) encapsulates the view of many who are concerned by this trend:

> [The] deployment of statistical measures tends to replace political debate with technical expertise [and] the growing reliance on indicators provides an example of the dissemination of the corporate form of thinking and governance into broader social spheres. . . . [Further,] indicators typically conceal their political and theoretical origins and underlying theories of social change and activism. (S83–S84)

While we are not ourselves so pessimistic about quantitative data and the motives of their producers, we understand and appreciate many critiques of data-driven research and policymaking. For example, we agree that the transparency of data used in scholarship and policymaking is often poor. Schedler (2012) examines twenty-five cross-national political data sets and finds even the most basic information about the data to be absent, particularly with regards to information necessary for establishing reliability. Only four out of the twenty-five datasets state the number of coders used to produce the data, and only two out of twenty-five report reliability statistic scores (242–243). As a result of such situations, data and the motives of their producers could certainly appear opaque. However, we don't generally believe this opacity to be intentional or insidious. Schedler, for example, sees this as a "regulatory problem" in that data is a growth industry with no controls or standards.

Further, we agree that not every question is appropriately answered with a quantitative approach. However, the same holds true for the qualitative approach. Often a mix of these two methods provides the best answer to socio-political research questions. The United Nations Development Programme and UN Women are prominent examples of entities that regularly engage in mixed-methods research, using both case-study and data-driven approaches.

In defense of a data-driven approach to scholarship, not all the problems ascribed to data are unique to data. We assert that quantitative data and qualitative prose and speech share certain key liabilities equally. In response to Merry (2011), we ask, "Is it not true that prose and speech, as well as data, can be opaque or simplistic; have hidden or explicit theoretical, ideological, and/or political motives; achieve prominence despite apparently evident faults; or can be summoned on behalf of either justice or repression?" Certainly, it is so.

We are taught from an early age how to differentiate some speech and prose from other speech and prose. It follows that, especially in this age of "big data," users of data and consumers of data-driven products (such as the ever-present infographics in news stories) have a duty to be educated about what they are using/consuming. Academics, laypersons, and especially policymakers must focus not only on what stories given data tell, but also on where those data came from, what information they contain, how much of this information they contain, and the reliability and validity of the data. With data, as with food, you are what you eat.

A further critique of the quantitative approach is that "some quantitative measures . . . are presented in terms of global maps. These quantitative measures enable quick comparisons. . . . In contrast, anthropologists argue that variations in phenomena such as freedom or rule of law are more complicated than that" (Hardin 2013). We understand this to mean that quantitative indicators tell stories about the world that are divorced from the context in which these stories take place, limiting our ability to understand what is under study. For single-indicator global maps, that is at least partly true. However, people do not necessarily view maps without incorporating context of their own. When a person looks at a map of the world indicating corruption or wealth at the country level, he or she likely incorporates pre-existing understandings of history and regime type into these maps. The knowledge and ideological baggage we normally bring to bear in understanding things presented to us does not disappear because a map is based on a number. Further, single-variable maps are typically more about generating questions than providing answers: Why are Northern Africa and Southwest Asia one color, but South America another color? That simple question could lead someone down many paths—qualitative, quantitative, or both—in the search for an answer.

Further, we note that quantitative data are often, and most correctly, interpreted using context. When statistical analyses such as those in this book are conducted, secondary data are employed to provide context for the stories the main data tell. These secondary data are often called *control variables*. Quantitative data can provide systematic context at the macro level (regime type, wealth, physical geography, population size, advocacy work, treaty obligations, domestic conflict, and countless more topics). Likewise, quantitative data can provide rich systematic context at the micro level, especially in survey data (age, education, party identification, knowledge about politics, health, work, experience with violence, military experience, experience with animals, and the like).

Tickner (2006, 37) notes that the reasons most feminist scholars of international relations have "avoided quantitative methods" include the following:

The choices that states make about which data to collect is a political act. Traditional ways in which data are collected and analyzed do not lend themselves to answering many of the questions feminists raise. The data that are available to scholars and, more importantly, the data that are not, determine which research questions get asked and how they are answered.

We agree with all three of these statements. In fact, they can be extended beyond state activity to that of large interstate organizations with institutionalized gender-related programs, such as the United Nations. The UN has passed many resolutions condemning violence against women. In 1993 the General Assembly passed the Declaration on the Elimination of Violence against Women, followed by further resolutions in 2006, 2007, and 2009, all with the aim to intensify efforts to eliminate all forms of VAW. The UN Security Council passed resolution 1325 in 2000 in an effort to address violence against women in armed conflict, and in 2008 the Security Council passed resolution 1820, which addressed sexual violence against women in conflict. Yet despite these resolutions and the existence of gender-specific treaties, violence against women has *not* been a systematic part of UN development reports' statistical tables, nor was it a component in its gender-empowerment measure (GEM), the Gender-Related Development Index (GDI), or the current Gender Inequality Index (GII).

At the same time, however, we don't think any of these concerns logically preclude conducting sound quantitative research on issues of interest to feminists—and in particular, violence against women. Tickner's three points pertain to a world where all data are generated by governments that have been "constituted historically as gendered entities" (38). We certainly don't contest the gendered history of government or the effects of this on what governments do and don't do. However, we do believe that as governments are increasingly not the only data producers in circulation, Tickner's critique ebbs in strength. If anything, rather than a reason to avoid data, Tickner's list of issues could be considered a wake-up call about the need for more nongovernmental data creation to diversify the research questions about women's lives that can be appropriately studied quantitatively. Indeed, the creation of independent, transparent data to address human rights issues not previously available for quantitative study is, we feel, a form of activism.

Why Measure Legal Guarantees?

The measures of legal guarantees, enforcement, and societal discrimination we introduce in this chapter contribute to an ever-expanding universe of data related to violence against women—an important effort for both scholars and activists. The United Nations Division for the Advancement of Women (UNIFEM, now UN Women) stated that systematic measures of violence against women can "help raise awareness" of the issue, "contribute to monitoring of progress in achieving goals" (of organizations and states), "contribute to policy evaluation" (of organizations and states), and "enable evidence-based comparison of trends over time, within and between countries" (UNDAW 2007, 19–20). Currently, however, there exist few data, and no systematic data of which we are aware, for evaluating the extent and scope of legal guarantees protecting women from violence globally. This is mostly a result of the great variability in data-collection practices among states, including inconsistency in the forms of violence for which information is collected and the variability in legal guarantees adopted at the national level. Thus, a UN Expert Group–written report titled "Indicators to Measure Violence against Women" recommended the development of standards that would be "a positive contribution to strengthening the knowledge base on violence against women" so that what happens in countries can be systematically monitored (UNDAW 2007, 19). Hudson et al. (2012, 106) go further in stating unequivocally that data such as these are necessary for important work linking the security of women with that of states.

What Data Already Exist?

Some data measuring the presence of VAW-related laws already exist. Here we review these data and explain any weaknesses that informed the construction of our own data.

UN Secretary General's Database on Violence against Women

The UN hosts an online database intended to provide vital information regarding violence against women, in an effort to "establish a coordinated database on the extent, nature, and consequences of all forms of violence against women" (UNDAW 2009). Unfortunately, this database provides incomplete coverage of those legal guarantees that are in existence, particularly for less developed countries. In addition, the UN database uses states parties' reports to human rights bodies and responses from member states to questionnaires as its sole source material, and this can be problematic. First, the types of information gathered are not systematic, as states decide themselves which items to report. Therefore, the reports lack uniformity on legal guarantees. Also, with respect CEDAW compliance, there are issues with nonreporting and overdue reports, and in some circumstances, states are allowed to combine reports from various years (Bayefsky 2001, 7).

Progress of the World's Women Reports

The United Nations Entity for Gender Equality and the Empowerment of Women, UN Women, releases a triennial themed report called *Progress of the World's Women* that includes some information regarding the progress of violence against women globally. These reports include information on the presence of marital-rape and sexual harassment laws in different regions of the world. For a few reasons, we do not use these data in our own work. For example, Figure 1.5 in the 2011–2012 *Progress of the World's Women: In Pursuit of Justice* (UNIFEM 2012, 33) shows, by world region, data about domestic violence, sexual harassment, and marital-rape laws. Annex 4 of the report gives country-specific information about the same. However, the measurement scheme used is dichotomous, meaning legislation is simply noted as either existing or not existing. We believe a dichotomous scheme cannot sufficiently represent the reality of variations in VAW-related laws as they exist in practice. This is because in practice laws differ in their strength; indeed, some are clearly designed to be ineffective in ameliorating violence against women. Thus, important variation in the strength of violence laws exists across forms of violence, across countries, and even within countries.[1]

The difference between what information can be provided by dichotomous and polychotomous (more than two categories) measurement schemes is important. For example, a country requiring the victims of domestic violence to use assault-and-battery laws (a "correlative law" situation in our scheme)[2] is quite different from one where explicit criminalization of domestic violence exists (a "full guarantee" situation). Further, coding legal guarantees dichotomously could distort reality such that a country with a notable level of actual legal protections would get placed in the same category as a country where it is a crime for women to report abuse. Situations like these are substantively unequal with regard to legal protections against VAW, and our measures need to reflect these differences. For example, Denmark's rape law allows a perpetrator of rape to escape punishment by marrying his victim. The consequences of such laws can be tragic: "In March 2012, a 16-year-old girl named Amina Filali killed herself by drinking rat poison. She had been raped and forced—by Moroccan law—to marry the man who had raped her" (McDaniel 2013). Yet in a dichotomous scheme such as UN Women's, Denmark and Morocco would count as "having a law."[3]

The 2011–2012 *Progress of the World's Women* report indicates Senegal has a law against sexual harassment. This appears to be true, and there is a considerable penalty for violation. However, the law is evidently written such that victims "found it difficult, if not impossible, to present sufficient proof to secure prosecutions" (US Department of State 2009e). Further, the Swiss good-governance and security organization the Geneva Centre for the Democratic Control of Armed Forces goes so far in a recent report on Senegal as to state there's no discernible harassment law. The Geneva Centre interviewed a Senegalese tribunal head who pointed to the incomplete, very narrow prohibition on sexual discrimination in the penal code (Reeves 2011, 213) as being the only active law addressing sexual harassment—indicating that, for all practical purposes, no legal protections existed. What good is a punishment for a crime that requires such a high standard of proof that average victims have no actual recourse? And what good is a law that is so bad that heads of tribunals do not even recognize their existence?

CEELI's CEDAW Assessment Tool

The American Bar Association Central and East European Law Initiative (CEELI) developed a CEDAW Assessment Tool in 2002 in an effort to measure the degree to which a nation's laws protect women's rights, specifically freedom from violence. However, since 2002 this tool has been utilized in only about a dozen states, limiting its utility.

OECD Social Institutions and Gender Index

In 2009, the Organisation for Economic Co-operation and Development (OECD) introduced its Social Institutions and Gender Index (SIGI) (OECD Development Centre 2012a). This is an ambitious project that offers, among other things, a large number of indicators across a broad spectrum of topics, a high degree of transparency in its sourcing of information, and a relatively high degree of transparency in its methodology.

The SIGI combines fourteen separate indicators that cover five dimensions of women's well-being. One of the indicators is "Violence against Women," which is an average of scores across three subcomponents: laws, attitudes toward domestic violence, and lifetime prevalence of domestic violence. Most relevant to our own endeavors in this book is the laws indicator. A country's score on laws is the average of its scores on the existence of three types of laws—sexual assault or rape, domestic violence, and sexual harassment—scored on the following scale (OECD Development Centre 2012b):

0: There is specific legislation in place

0.25: There is specific legislation in place, but there are widespread reported problems with implementation

0.5: There is general legislation in place, or specific legislation is inadequate (e.g. rape laws do not criminalise marital rape)

0.75: Legislation is being planned, drafted or reviewed or existing legislation is highly inadequate

1: No legislation

Despite the many strengths of the SIGI project, several issues in its "laws" measure lead us to reject it for our own use in studying the presence and strength of VAW laws. First, and most importantly to us, the "laws" measure aggregates law and practice into a single score. We prefer law and practice to be addressed separately in measures, as the factors that explain law and practice differ, as do the independent consequences of law and practice. Further, the SIGI measure aggregates laws relating to different forms of violence against women into the same score. To use this measure in statistical analyses, then, one would have to make the assumption that the factors that relate to the implementation and enforcement of all kinds of VAW laws are identical. Our analyses in the following chapter show that this is not the case. Further, the implementation component to the SIGI "laws" measure is dichotomous. In reality, laws aren't simply enforced or not enforced—there is great variety in levels of enforcement. We outline our own measure of enforcement of VAW laws in Appendix A.

Further, we disagree that countries planning legislation should be given credit for something that has not happened yet. However, we do not know the parameters for what counts as planning for purposes of the SIGI measure. Politics is a graveyard of good (and bad) ideas that died at conception. If one legislator proposes a bill that gets reviewed by committee but goes nowhere, does that count here? If a bill is voted down, session after session, does that count here?

And more importantly, do either of these situations merit saying law exists in any form? The OECD measure implies that they do, and we disagree.

Finally, there is a lack of transparency with the weighting scheme. For example, a country that has well-enforced general legislation in place is given half the score of a country with unenforced specific legislation. Evidently, strength of legislation is weighted more heavily in this measure than is enforcement. However, we know neither how much so or on what these weights are based.

WomanStats

The WomanStats database is a repository for cross-national data and information on women, containing more than 320 variables for 175 countries on the situation and status of women internationally (Hudson et al. 2012). The value of this project to scholars, policymakers, and advocates is beyond question. However, much as the WomanStats project improved upon the three women's-rights indicators originally provided by the CIRI Human Rights Data Project (Cingranelli and Richards 2010), we believe the legal data created for this book to be an improvement upon correlative data from the WomanStats project.

Our legal data differ both in approach and substance from those in the WomanStats project. The primary WomanStats indicator with a legal component germane to our endeavor is "Multivariate Scale #1 (Physical Security of Women)."[4] Like the OECD's SIGI, this indicator mixes law and enforcement of the law. However, this measure also includes societal practice. Most importantly, however, the WomanStats scale assumes a cumulative pattern of the granting of legal guarantees. The asserted pattern is as such across the five scale points:

> 0: There are laws against domestic violence, rape, and marital rape
> 1: There are laws against domestic violence, rape, and marital rape
> 2: There are laws against domestic violence, rape, and marital rape
> 3: There are laws against domestic violence, rape, but not necessarily marital rape
> 4: There are no or weak laws against domestic violence, rape, and marital rape[5]

This pattern asserts three things. First, there are only three patterns of the existence of these legal guarantees across countries:

> A. There are laws against domestic violence, rape, and marital rape.
> B. There are laws against domestic violence and rape, but not necessarily marital rape.

C. There are no or weak laws against domestic violence, rape, and marital rape.

Second, because this pattern is embedded within an ordinal scale, it is assumed that countries universally move from pattern C to pattern A, in that order. While it makes sense that countries would move from having no laws to having a full set of laws, it does not make sense that the only interesting type of legal variation is from having no laws to having laws, and that marital rape is the only type of law for which there is interesting variation within a country over time, or across countries. As Cingranelli and Richards (1999) point out, such patterns are empirically testable, and our analyses later in this book will test the sequencing of VAW-related legal guarantees.

Finally, the WomanStats scale pattern asserts that having weak laws is the same as having no laws at all. We would disagree, and will show in our discussion of rape law that follows, as well as our analyses, that there is great variation in what might be considered a weak law.

How Do We Measure Legal Guarantees against Four Forms of Violence against Women?

In this section we describe the creation of our original legal data indicating the strength of domestic legal guarantees against four forms of violence in 196 countries from 2007 through 2010. The four forms of violence included are rape, spousal rape, domestic violence, and sexual harassment.[6] We chose these four forms from among the many others because it was for these four that cross-national information was most available. We wish to be clear that our choice of these four forms of gender-based violence is not a judgment about their effect on human dignity relative to other forms. Quite the contrary; we hope others might use our approach to data creation to extend the list of indicators to cover all forms.

The Coding Scheme

From our studies of real-world variation in domestic legal guarantees relating to violence against women, we created a four-point ordinal coding scheme for the strength of domestic legal guarantees addressing VAW:

Legal guarantees prohibiting [*type of violence against women*] are
0 Nonexistent/Discriminatory
1 Incomplete/Weak
2 Correlative
3 Fully Provided For

0: Nonexistent/Discriminatory

A country receives a score of 0 if there are no laws prohibiting the form of violence against women being considered. Instances where a country's code of law is based on traditions that are fundamentally biased against women also receive a score of 0. For example, this situation might arise when a country bases its legal system on certain interpretations of Sharia that automatically disadvantage women. However, to receive a score of 0, discriminatory interpretations of the law must be applied specifically to the form of violence being considered. Also, countries in which there exists a law excusing one of the four forms of violence against women considered in this dimension receive a score of 0 for legal guarantees concerning that form of violence. To legally excuse means to either absolve completely or provide for significantly light sentencing. For example, in many countries a rape victim can be forced to marry her rapist, who then goes unpunished, having married his victim. Further, countries where women face punishment or possible prosecution for reporting any of the four legal guarantees included in this dimension are coded a 0 for legal guarantees regarding that form of violence.

Finally, if the only existing law pertaining to violence against women is a constitutional provision stating that discrimination against women is illegal, the country receives a score of 0 for that form of violence, so long as it fails to explicitly forbid any form of violence against women. In cases where it is specifically mentioned or it is reasonable to infer that a government elevates statutory laws, penal codes, customary laws, and other laws over the country's constitution, the coding decision is based solely upon these laws and not the constitution. The rationale behind this rule is that in most countries statutes often contain discriminatory regulations that contradict constitutional provisions.

1: Incomplete/Weak Laws

A country receives a score of 1 if a law exists that prohibits one of the four forms of violence considered in this measure but the law is incomplete or limited in scope. For example, legal guarantees prohibiting a form of violence are considered incomplete/weak if they do not extend to women in one or more minority groups. A country would also receive a score of 1 if customary law that is contradictory to national statutes prohibiting one of the four forms of violence takes precedence in one or more minority groups. A country, such as the United Arab Emirates in 2008, that prohibits a specific form of violence but does not recognize that form of violence in Sharia courts, receives a score of 1 because of the de facto power of Sharia courts in that country.

Also, countries where one of the four forms of violence against women is prohibited but the burden of proof is unduly placed upon the female accuser receive a score of 1 for legal guarantees regarding a specific form of violence. For example, the 2008 US State Department Country Report for Argentina states, "Rape, including spousal rape, is a crime, but the need for proof, either in the form of clear physical injury or the testimony of a witness, often presented difficulties" (US Department of State 2009a).

A country may receive at most a score of 1 in cases where the law provides for systematic light or reduced sentencing for a perpetrator of one of the four forms of violence. Reasons given for systematic light/reduced sentencing may include cases where if the victim chooses to marry or remain with a perpetrator, he receives no punishment. This can be the case where national law allows tradition/custom to trump its authority. For example, in Morocco, "While not provided for by law, victim's families may offer marriage as an alternative to rapists to preserve family honor" (US Department of State 2009d).

A country where laws exist against any of the four forms of violence considered in this dimension, but a source indicates that those laws are written so as to be unenforceable and/or difficult to apply, receives a 1 for legal guarantees concerning that form of violence against women. Laws are often written so as to be unenforceable or difficult to apply when the law is not defined and the source indicates that state agents were unable to enforce the law because of the way it was written. Unenforceability might arise from overly narrow legal definitions. Rape, for example, is often subjected to a narrow "mechanical" conceptualization. We do not employ such a mechanical definition in rating laws addressing rape, however. In its judgment in the landmark case of *Prosecutor v. Akayesu*,[7] the International Criminal Tribunal for Rwanda "sought to ensure that the fundamentally aggressive nature of the act of rape should not be eclipsed by a mechanical obsession with what needs to be done (e.g. penetration) with which body parts," and instead emphasized that "rape represents a violation of personal dignity, which can be used to intimidate, degrade, humiliate, discriminate, punish, control or destroy a person" (Munro 2010, 17). Unfortunately, as Cole (2010, 54) points out, the legal battles resulting from a mechanical definition of rape are typically solely about whether a victim consented, and this "can be problematic since the factual circumstances of rape usually do not permit the discovery of corroborating evidence such as additional witnesses." In *Are Women Human?* (2006), Catherine MacKinnon makes a strong argument against mechanical definitions of rape and notes that many societies have varying understandings of consent and coercion, and therefore in places where severe male control over females is part of everyday life, one will never find mechanical consent, as the consent is itself a form of psychological violence (coercion) that's been perpetrated on women en masse through traditions/norms.

Finally, a country receives a score of 1 if there are laws against one of the four forms of violence in this dimension, but a source indicates that these legal guarantees fail to address all components of that specific form of violence. This might be, for example, a domestic violence law that does not allow for the issuance of restraining orders.

2: CORRELATIVE LAWS

In certain instances, countries utilize laws to prohibit particular forms of violence against women but do not mention these forms of violence by name. If no laws specifically prohibit a form of violence against women but other laws applied in practice effectively prohibit this form of violence, then a country receives a score of 2. These laws should both function as correlative to legal guarantees that explicitly forbid a given form of violence against women and be utilized in practice. For example, in Burundi "the law does not specifically prohibit domestic violence; however, persons accused of domestic violence can be tried under assault provisions" (US Department of State 2008c).

We treat correlative laws as lower in stature than explicit guarantees because one of the most important factors in the violation of human rights is the ascription of some groups of persons as less than human. Women certainly are treated this way, and have been throughout history. The creation of explicit guarantees of violence against women denotes the special and specific nature of this form of human rights abuse and sends important messages to society at large about women as humans. Further, it is representative of larger socio-legal norms that must be present for the passing of explicit guarantees. For those reasons, we think that countries able and willing to produce explicit guarantees are further along the continuum of progressive realization than those that apply correlative laws in practice. An example of the use of correlative laws is Tajikistan, a state that drafted a bill on domestic violence in 2003 but has yet to pass the law. Tajikistan criminal code outlaws physical assault and injury generally, but experts say "the absence of protections and penalties for violence in the home undermines efforts to support victims (Kurbanova 2010). The government might be reluctant to take action in passing this specific bill because the family domain is viewed as part of a very private sphere in Tajikistan. The passage of specific laws protecting women from violence is necessary to raise awareness of violence and protect victims. Specifically, in the environment of Tajikistan, where violence against women is considered a private matter, "a domestic violence law is especially necessary to spell out the nature of such offences and the fact that they are actually crimes" (ibid.). A notable exception is that where an incomplete correlative law exists, the country is scored a 1 rather than a 2 because scope trumps mere de facto legal institution in a de jure measure.

3: FULLY PROVIDED FOR

A country should receive a score of 3 if the form of violence against women being considered is legally prohibited. To receive a score of 3, a source should directly state that the country's laws explicitly forbid the type of violence being considered. A 3 implies that all persons are covered by law. The creation of *explicit* prohibitions of violence against women denotes the special and specific nature of this form of human rights abuse and sends important messages to society at large about women as humans (see MacKinnon 2006). Additionally, a country's having explicit guarantees is representative of larger socio-legal norms that must be present for the passing of those guarantees. For those reasons, countries with explicit guarantees are further along the continuum of protection of women's dignity than those that merely apply correlative laws in practice.

Information Sources

Scores of information sources were used to create our legal-guarantees data. We examined so many sources because often different sources, *and sometimes the same source,* can provide conflicting information. Thus the use of multiple sources to create data is a common strategy to reduce the amount of bias that can be introduced by a single source of information.[8] We began by planning to use the annual US State Department Country Reports on Human Rights Practices as our primary information source (US Department of State, Annual). This report is the largest and most-systematic human rights report available. By "systematic," we mean that each report provides information about government respect for the same set of internationally recognized human rights for each country, and for every country in the world. No other report is as comprehensive, and because these reports also use information culled from a multitude of domestic and international advocacy groups, they have achieved some authoritative stature.

The State Department's human rights reports contain gender-related information for each country, and there is a specific subsection on women within the "Discrimination, Societal Abuses, and Trafficking in Persons" section for each country. This subsection contains a good deal of information about, among other things, the prevalence of violence toward women, laws addressing this violence, attitudes about gender-based violence, and the strength of enforcement of any laws. At first glance this would seem a perfect source of information for creating our measures, and we did use these reports when creating our data. Having a similar amount of information about the same rights for each country goes a long way in reducing bias in our measurements due to uneven information across different rights or countries.

Ultimately, however, we did not use the State Department human rights reports as the authoritative source from which to create our data for this book. It became clear that for a near majority of the cases in our dataset, the reports contained misleading and/or factually inaccurate information regarding VAW-related legislation. One result of such inaccuracies is that where we saw changes in a country's scores from year to year, these would often be the result of error rather than of actual changes in the phenomenon being measured (such as legal guarantees). For example, the 2007 and 2008 reports for Saint Lucia state that "rape, including spousal rape, is a crime punishable by 14 years' to life imprisonment" (US Department of State 2008b, 2009c). However, the 2009 report states that "the law effectively criminalizes rape, but not spousal rape" (US Department of State 2010b). This would seem to indicate the retraction of a spousal-rape statute. Given this inconsistency, we went to the text of the law and found spousal rape is illegal only where a *decree nisi* of divorce is in effect. Thus, there existed at best an *incomplete* law against marital rape.

At times the State Department Country Reports were simply completely wrong. For example, the reports on Nigeria state that "the law recognizes spousal rape as a separate offense" (US Department of State 2008a, 2009b, 2010a, and 2011). However, spousal rape is explicitly allowed in Nigeria's penal code. Nigeria's Criminal Code Act, Part 1, Chapter 1, Paragraph 6, states "'unlawful carnal knowledge' means carnal connection which takes place otherwise than between husband and wife" (Nigeria 2013). Indeed, Section 282 of Nigeria's penal code states that "a husband cannot be charged with marital rape" (UNDAW 2013). In the case of

Swaziland, the State Department reported as early as 2007 that marital rape had been criminalized. However, a 2011 submission to Swaziland's Universal Periodic Review by the Centre for Human Rights Faculty of Law, University of Pretoria, asserted that "in Swaziland, there are no laws criminalising marital rape. The Girls and Women's Protection Act 39 of 1920 which is still in force is silent on the matter. Men can sexually abuse their wives and have done so without fear of sanctions. Spousal rape has become a common occurrence in Swaziland" (University of Pretoria Centre 2011). In late October 2011, Swaziland's lower legislative house passed the Sexual Offences and Domestic Violence Bill of 2009, which would outlaw marital rape, but it still has not been signed into law as of August 2014.

So, instead of the State Department Country Reports, we ended up using the following types of sources, listed in order of most to least authoritative:

1. Criminal codes/penal codes
2. Case law
3. UN-based resources
4. Nongovernmental organization (NGO) reports
5. News accounts

Many times these types of sources reinforced one another. For example, case law and UN/NGO reports were useful in both alerting us to the presence of many laws, as well as clarifying the actual nature of some vague laws.

Whenever possible, we turned to statutory provisions. This was complicated by both imperfect availability of laws and the availability of countries' laws in English. Greatly helpful in this endeavor was the *Foreign Law Guide* (Reynolds and Flores 2012). This subscription database contains updated statutory code and constitutional content of all kinds for almost every country in the world. To do so, it relies on more than fifty other databases of information about constitutions and statutes.[9] Many of these databases are regional. For instance, the Office for Democratic Institutions and Human Rights of the Organization for Security and Cooperation in Europe runs a website called Legislationline that provides up-to-date statutes about the organization's member states.[10] Others are themed, providing information on business, environmental, or health law. Not all kinds of laws were available for all countries in this source, however, so we conduced systematic Internet searches over the course of several years to find laws not in the *Foreign Law Guide*.

We frequently used news stories from around the world to gain information about the status of gender violence–based legal guarantees. Both the LexisNexis database and Google News searches proved invaluable for these tasks. Often, advocacy-group statements would point us to the fact that a law on the books was, in actuality, unenforceable and/or otherwise useless as written. For instance, in consultations preparing for the 57th Session of the UN Commission on the Status of Women, Ghanaian women's groups expressed displeasure that Ghana's Ministry of Women and Children Affairs had not done enough to pass the legislative instrument necessary for implementing the country's five-year-old Domestic Violence Act (*Ghana Business News* 2012). Such accounts provided crucial information about how a collective of societal groups working with a particular law on a regular basis would view its worth.

One must be careful when using news sources, however, as they may hold incomplete truths and/or biases. In researching Hungary, one might encounter a story about how a corporate entity (in this case, the United States–based Avon) partnered with domestic NGOs to circulate a petition asking the government to criminalize domestic violence (Jovanavski 2012). Taking that at face value, one's conclusion would be that there is no law protecting victims of domestic violence. Here, the importance of multisourcing data becomes clear. A presentation by Hungary's Office of Justice at the 2010 European Seminar on Domestic Violence noted that while domestic violence does not have a distinct status in Hungary's legal code, "there are nearly 30 legal statuses in the Criminal Code and in the Act on misdemeanors which include physical, psychological and sexual abuse or negligence and thus fall under the category of [domestic violence]" (Tòth 2010, slide 3). The presentation also cited Act LXXII of 2009 on Restraining Orders because of Violence between Relatives as addressing domestic violence. The UN Women data in the 2011–2012 *Progress of the World's Women* (UN Women 2012) reports Hungary as having no domestic violence law. That is true in a nominal sense. However, there *are* specific laws that address the consequences of domestic violence, so Hungary shouldn't be put in the same category as, say, Iraq or Iran. Our multicategory scheme allows Hungary to be placed in the category of "correlative laws."

Rape and Marital-Rape Law: A Mini Case Study

Our experience in coding the strength of rape laws and marital-rape laws is illustrative of the difficulties in creating measures of legal guarantees. These methodological difficulties reflect the complexities faced by advocates trying to improve women's recourse to legal justice in cases of sexual violence. What follows highlights a few of the issues to be dealt with in gauging the strength of rape and marital-rape laws.

To measure the strength of rape laws in countries around the world, one must first grapple with the issue of what constitutes rape for legal purposes. Not all countries use the term *rape,* opting instead for the concept of *sexual assault* as is suggested by the UN Model Legislation on sexual violence. These guidelines suggest replacing "existing offences of rape and 'indecent' assault with a broad offence of sexual assault graded based on harm" (UNDAW 2010, 26). This recognizes rape as one class of sexual assault. A 2009 report by the Committee on Equal Opportunities for Women and Men of the Council of Europe's Parliamentary Assembly suggests its member states explicitly make rape an ex officio crime (one where the victim need not press charges for the case to be pursued by authorities), but also makes it clear that rape is regarded as one among various types of sexual violence (Council of Europe 2009, 2). One rationale for a graded *sexual assault* scheme rather than a crime of *rape* itself is based on the fact that rape laws in many places are quite mechanical. For example, they might mandate the nonconsensual penetration of a female's specific sex organ by the specific sex organ of a male. In Chapter 18 of Tonga's criminal code, what the law calls "carnal knowledge" specifically requires penetration of the vagina by a penis for an act to constitute rape (Article 118). Sodomy is dealt with separately, and discusses "emission of seed" in its evidentiary language (Article 140).

Simple, seemingly intuitive definitions of rape, such as "sexual intercourse without consent" (Hawkesworth 2012, 127), useful for some discursive purposes, can lead to mechanical conceptualizations when applied to the endeavor of creating legislation. Laws that are overly mechanical in their construction of what actions constitute crimes can shut off avenues of justice for victims of some acts. That is, mechanical or cataloguing approaches to violence-related law can leave out many manners in which violations can occur, including violation of a victim's body apart from sexual organs with objects or body parts other than the perpetrator's sexual organs. Same-sex violations are also excluded. Indeed, one problem with both the Council of Europe report and the UN Model Legislation is that neither offers definitional guidance. The Council of Europe report does not define what should constitute rape for the purposes of legal proceedings. The UN legislation says rape should be discarded as a category, but offers only that sexual violence is a "violation of bodily integrity and sexual autonomy" (UNDAW 2010, 26). This, unfortunately, allows states a great deal of latitude to construct laws that they say pertain to sexual violence and/or rape, but are so mechanical as to be ineffectual or, actually, discriminatory.

Jurisprudence suffers, ultimately, in the presence of badly conceptualized laws. Decision Point 20 in *Sakshi v. Union of India*[11] upheld Section 375 of the Indian Penal Code stating that an allegation of rape has to satisfy the following criteria:

I. Sexual intercourse between a man with a woman in the following circumstances: (a) against the will of the woman; (b) without her consent; (c) under duress; (d) consent obtained by fraud; (e) consent obtained by reason of unsoundness of mind or intoxication.

II. If the woman is below the age of 16 years, sexual intercourse is deemed to amount to rape. Even if the woman has consented, it would be considered rape under the law.

III. There is however, an exception to this definition of rape. Un-consented sexual intercourse between a man and his wife would not amount to rape if the wife is 16 years or older [at the time of decision].

This mechanistic decision offered no help in later cases, such as *Tara Dutt v. State*,[12] in which a fifty-four-year old man was charged with digitally violating a disabled five-year-old girl whose mother was related to him. From 1860 to February 2013, the criminal law of India did not recognize this as rape or even as a "heinous sexual assault." Instead of rape, India's law called the sexual violation of a child by and with a grown man's hands "outraging the modesty of a woman" under Section 354 of the penal code. India is by no means alone in this regard. Attacking the legitimacy of the concept of date rape in the United States, equality feminist Christina Hoff Summers "dismisse[d] the notion that forcible penetration by a finger or other object should count as sexual assault" (Meloy and Miller 2011, 32–33).

Mechanical laws can get quite specific, even governing the extent of penetration. The Democratic Republic of the Congo's penal code uses the term "however slightly" with regard to the extent of penetration necessary for a rape to occur. In Indian rape trials, "the finger test" is "a practice where the examining doctor notes the presence or absence of the hymen and the size and so-called laxity of the vagina of the rape survivor. The finger test is supposed to assess whether girls and women are 'virgins' or 'habituated to sexual intercourse'" (Human Rights Watch 2010, 2–3). The implication, of course, is that women who have been sexually active are treated differently than virgins when rape cases are brought to trial. In the trial of Mohammed Jaffar, charged with raping a six-year-old girl, the examining doctor testified that "the hymen orifice admitted tip of little finger . . . and the vaginal orifice admits one finger with difficulty" (30). This testimony convinced the court that Jaffar did not penetrate the girl's vagina with his penis and charges were reduced to "attempt to rape." Had penetration occurred, it would have been rape, so a dichotomous rape-law measure would score India as a "yes" for having a law, with no ability to denote the great weakness of the law in the measure.

Legal codes making rape a crime against modesty or chastity are undesirable because they are not based on the injury to the female victim herself, but rather on rape as a degradation of the female as property of a male or as an insult upon decent society. Mayer (2013, 106) offers a strong human rights–related critique of what she calls fundamentalist Islam's "obsession with chastity," stating that "the obsession with preserving women's chastity can justify a policy of locking women up in their homes" whereby "respect for their chastity is a principle used to restrict women's freedoms." The separate and lesser crime of impinging upon a woman's modesty or chastity is, unfortunately, not rare in societies where tradition/religion/custom have a strong influence on national/state statutes, or where national/state statutes explicitly allow for the legal predominance of tradition/religion/custom. Law can begin to change the societal role of women in this regard, however. The Philippines had a similar class of crime called "crimes against chastity," but changed its law in 2004 with the Anti–Violence against Women and Their Children Act. Rape is now punishable by *reclusion perpetua*. This act even prohibits mediation/conciliation of cases at the village level (a clear acknowledgement of tradition/custom as a source of discrimination).

Consent is another concept that can be overly mechanically ascribed in statute. Laws vary in the extent to which victims must demonstrate a rape was nonconsensual, including allowing courts to begin cases with the presumption of female consent and/or requiring victims to demonstrate they struggled physically to resist a rapist. For example, in South Carolina a woman testified her husband dragged her by the throat into a bedroom, tied her hands and legs, put duct tape on her eyes and mouth, and put stockings and a garter belt on her legs. He then turned on a videotape recorder and filmed himself having intercourse with her. South Carolina's marital-rape law required physical proof of abuse, and, indeed, the husband was found in a van an hour after the rape with the videotape, video camera, and other items used in the encounter. "No, I didn't rape my wife. How can you rape your own wife?" the husband testified in court, adding that he did not think his wife was serious when she said "no" (Soto 1992, 4A). The defense lawyer argued consent was implicit because, as he stated, "the woman enjoyed watching pornographic movies" (Houston Chronicle News Services 1992, 3). The judge blocked attempts by the prosecution to call to the stand the husband's former wife so that she could give testimony about being tied and raped by the same man. The husband was acquitted. How strong is a law that allows courts to employ presumptive consent? Just knowing whether there is a law, or even that there is a specific law, tells us nothing in this regard.

The level of legal detail into which one could go when rating countries' rape laws can become almost dizzying. For example, how far should a "full legal guarantee" extend? Were a victim to conceive as a result of rape and then carry the child to term, should the rapist hold parental rights? Half the states in the United States have no protection for the mothers of children conceived from rape, and two have protections that apply only where the victim is a minor or a stepchild/adopted child of the rapist (Prewitt 2010). Of the twenty-five states that do have legal protections, thirteen require conviction for a rapist to lose parental privileges, which is a problem in several regards. First, only 0.2 to 5.2 percent of all rapes committed end in a conviction of the rapist, so this means too many women end up being forced to coexist, in some sense or other, with their attackers (Lonsway and Archambault 2012, 157). This complicates greatly, delays significantly, or even prevents psychological healing from the mental trauma of the rape. Second, rapists can use their custodial privilege to push a victim not to press charges in return for waiving legal rights to a child. Even a judge's decision whether to require an attacker to pay restitution (versus child support) affects the issue. In Massachusetts, for example, a rapist ordered to pay restitution loses parental privileges, while one ordered to pay child support does not.

The ideal measure of legal guarantees would incorporate information at this level of detail. However, the gathering of such detailed information across countries becomes almost impossible. Indeed, for many countries it was difficult enough to find enough information to corroborate a simple ordinal score such as in our measurement scheme. That's not at all to say, however, that a greater level of detail than what we present should not be aspired to. Quite the contrary: we truly hope our measures provoke discussion about improvement in both the measurement of legal guarantees relating to gender-based violence in particular, and the gathering of cross-national comparative legal data in general.

Conclusion

No *methodology* is without its benefits and drawbacks. While we agree with some of the critiques of data-driven research, we do not find any reason it cannot be carefully employed for a broad spectrum of socio-political research topics, including violence against women. No *measure* is without its benefits and drawbacks. From surveying the strengths and weaknesses of a variety of existing measures of legal guarantees, we learned a great deal about what we did and did not want to do in creating our own cross-national legal data. Our data are certainly not without their strengths and weaknesses, and we have carefully outlined many difficult choices we faced in creating these data so as to provide as much transparency as possible. Our data do not tell every story possible about VAW-related legal guarantees—no data could. However, we hope we've shown that we made every effort within our abilities to make the stories they do tell reliable and valid.

CHAPTER 5

❦

DISCOVERIES FROM OUR DATA

In this chapter, we explore what stories the data, whose creation we described in the previous chapter, tell us about legal protections relating to violence against women (VAW) around the world. The goal is to discover any information that might be of assistance to those looking to create/strengthen such laws where they are nonexistent/deficient. First, we use the data to describe the state of these laws around the world, both over time and across space. Then, we examine the relations between these legal protections themselves to ascertain whether there are any important regularities in how these laws are created. Last, we test our hypotheses about what socio-political factors are reliable associates of the presence and strength of gender-violence laws and whether the strength of VAW laws is predictive of outcomes related to the enhanced dignity of women.

General Patterns

Type and Time

Figure 5.1 shows the average level of legal protections against four forms of violence against women from 2007 to 2010, worldwide. First, let us compare the types of laws with one another. Rape is the form of violence against women having the strongest legal prohibitions on average, followed by domestic violence, sexual harassment, and marital rape, respectively. For example, the average score for rape across the time period is 2.55 out of 3.0, so we can report that the average country has full legal protections against the act of rape. On the other hand, the average score for marital rape across the time period is 1.17, indicating that the average country has incomplete or unenforceable legal protections against marital rape. Later in this chapter we explore why this is the case. Across time, these seem to be relatively stable results, as the relative strength of the frameworks is rather steady from 2007 to 2010.

There are two encouraging things to point out. First, change seems to be in a positive direction, as each of the four indicators shows a small bit of increase in strength on average during the period. Second, the improvement from 2007 to 2010 in legal protections against domestic violence worldwide is statistically significant. This means we can be almost certain that the improvement in the worldwide average from 1.84 in 2007 to 2.03 in 2010 is not due to chance alone. Keeping in mind, however, that the maximum possible score is 3.0, the dominant story from Figure 5.1 is that legal protections against three of these four forms of violence against women, unfortunately, have a long way to go toward being acceptable in any meaningful sense.

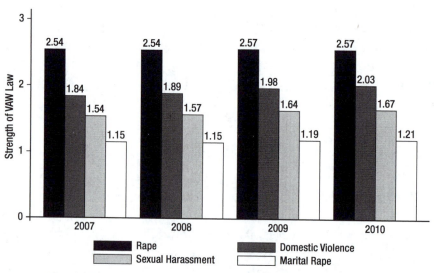

Figure 5.1 Average global legal strength scores, by year.

Space

What happens if we disaggregate our descriptive analysis by world region? Figure 5.2 shows the average regional level of legal protections against four forms of VAW from 2007 to 2010.[1] Europe and North America stand out as having the strongest legal regimes among these six regions. North America (comprised here of Canada and the United States) is the only region where sexual harassment laws were stronger than domestic violence laws. However, this is the result of having only two countries in the region, and one of them—Canada—having received a score of 2 (indicating the presence of a correlative law) for both domestic violence and marital rape.

The lowest legal protections among the six regions in Figure 5.2 were in Africa (fifty-two countries in our sample), Asia (fifty countries in our sample), and Oceania (fourteen countries in our sample). Oceania manifested the weakest protections against sexual harassment, while Asia had the weakest legal protections against rape, marital rape, and domestic violence. Table 5.1 shows the average subregional level of legal protections against the four forms of violence against women from 2007 to 2010. The information in Table 5.1 allows us to investigate what parts of these larger regions are most responsible for these weak

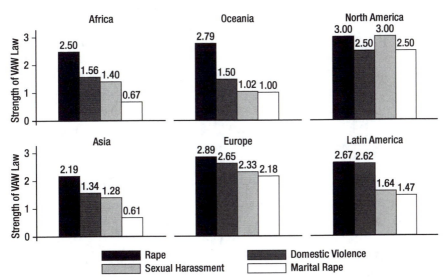

Figure 5.2   Average legal strength scores by region, 2007–2010.

Table 5.1 Average Legal Strength Scores by Subregion, 2007–2010

	Rape	Marital Rape	Domestic Violence	Sexual Harassment	Number of Countries
Australia/New Zealand	3	3	3	3	2
Caribbean	2.85	1.15	2.62	1.31	13
Central America	2.75	1.5	2.94	1.63	8
East Africa	2.82	0.7	2	1.55	18
East Asia	2.5	0.67	1.83	1.67	6
Eastern Europe	2.8	1.98	2.05	1.5	10
Melanesia	2.25	0.75	1.5	0.56	4
Micronesia	3	1	1.2	0.8	5
Mid-Africa	2.78	0.67	1.44	1.22	9
North Africa	1	0	1.2	1.6	5
North America	3	2.5	2.5	3	2
Northern Europe	2.8	2.3	2.45	2.8	10
Polynesia	3	0	1	0.67	3
South Africa	2.6	1.2	1.75	1.6	5
South America	2.42	1.79	2.42	2	12
Southern Europe	2.93	2.08	2.98	2.44	14
South-Central Asia	2.11	0.57	1.39	1.32	14
Southeast Asia	2.64	1.05	1.91	1	11
West Africa	2.44	0.69	1.23	1.22	16
West Asia	1.89	0.37	0.82	1.28	19
Western Europe	3	2.44	3	2.56	9

protections. In the case of Oceania, it is Melanesia, Micronesia, and Polynesia that are responsible for this region having the weakest average legal protections against sexual harassment. For example, the Federated States of Micronesia, Kiribati, Marshall Islands, Papua New Guinea, Samoa, Solomon Islands, and Vanuatu and all received scores of 0 (no law or discriminatory law) in 2010 on sexual harassment.

Western Asia was, by far, the single subregion most responsible for Asia having the weakest legal protections against rape, marital rape, and domestic violence. This can be seen best in Figures 5.3 through 5.6. The four maps can be read such that the lighter a country's color, the worse that country is regarding affording legal protections against VAW. The darker a country is on the map, the greater such legal protections have been afforded to citizens. On the map of rape laws (upper left), it's instantly clear that Western Asia and Northern Africa fail in providing legal protection of the sort seen nearly everywhere else in the world. Seven countries from the Western Asia subregion received a score of 0 (no law or discriminatory law) in 2010 on rape: Jordan, Lebanon, Kuwait, Saudi Arabia,

Syria, United Arab Emirates, and Yemen. Western Asia accounted for 44 percent of all countries, globally, receiving a 0 on rape in 2010.

The manner in which Western Asia and Northern Africa stand out in Figures 5.3 through 5.6 with regard to their minimal (if any) legal protections is striking. Western Asia accounted for 21 percent of the countries worldwide receiving a 0 for marital-rape laws in 2010. It accounted for 44 percent of the countries worldwide that received a 0 for legal protections against domestic violence in 2010. Western Asia's share of these poor scores is even more remarkable, as this subregion comprises only 10 percent of the countries in our data sample.

What is it about Western Asia that is responsible for these weak or absent legal protections? One important cultural commonality among the Western Asian states is that, with the exception of Armenia, Cyprus, Georgia, and Israel, they are majority Muslim (meaning that Islam is the religion of more than half the population). Figure 5.7 shows that, on average, states with a majority-Muslim population have far weaker legal protections against gender-based violence than states with citizenries of other majority-religion status.[2] While the difference between the two sets of countries in Figure 5.7 is startling, majority-Muslim status may not be the whole story. The subregions of East Africa, West Africa, and South-Central Asia also are dominantly composed of majority-Muslim states, but while their legal protections are weak relative to Europe, Latin America, and North America, their laws are much better than those of Western Asia. With the exception of Western Africa's score on sexual harassment, all of Western Asia falls behind these other regions in legal protections offered. On the other hand, the only subregion with worse legal protections is Northern Africa (Algeria, Libya, Morocco, Sudan, and Tunisia), and these are all majority-Muslim states.

Maybe the difference has nothing to do with the issue of gender-based violence, and Western Asia is simply less likely to adopt legal protections of any kind for any of its citizens. To briefly examine this possibility, we look at the difference between Western Asia and the other subregions (East Africa, North Africa, West Africa, and South-Central Asia) in how they score on the CIRI Human Rights Data Project's Empowerment Rights Index (Cingranelli and Richards 2010). This index combines each country's scores on seven indicators of substantive human rights protections: foreign movement, domestic movement, freedom of speech, freedom of assembly and association, workers' rights, electoral self-determination, and freedom of religion. It ranges from 0 (no government respect at all for these seven rights) to 14 (full government respect for these seven rights). Eighty-three percent of Western Asia scores in the lower half (0 to 6) of this index of protections. However, only 56 percent of the other four majority-Muslim regions score

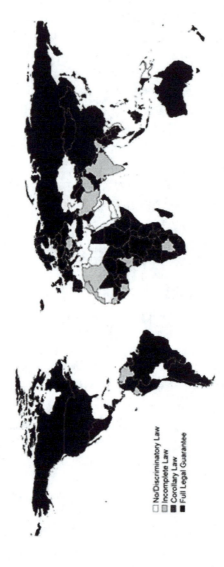

Figure 5.3   Global patterns of legal protections against rape, 2010.

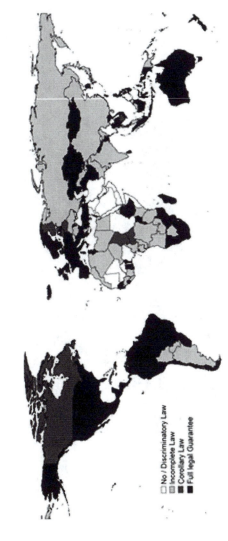

Figure 5.4   Global patterns of legal protections against domestic violence, 2010.

☐ No / Discriminatory Law
▨ Incomplete Law
▦ Corollary Law
■ Full legal Guarantee

Figure 5.5   Global patterns of legal protections against sexual harassment, 2010.

□ No / Discriminatory Law
▣ Incomplete Law
▦ Corollary Law
■ Full Legal Guarantee

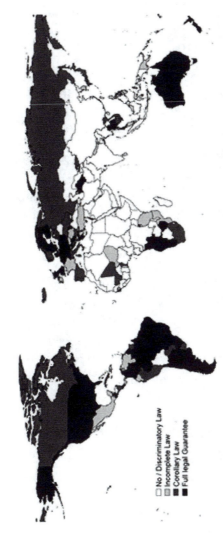

Figure 5.6   Global patterns of legal protections against marital rape, 2010.

□ No / Discriminatory Law
▨ Incomplete Law
■ Corollary Law
■ Full legal Guarantee

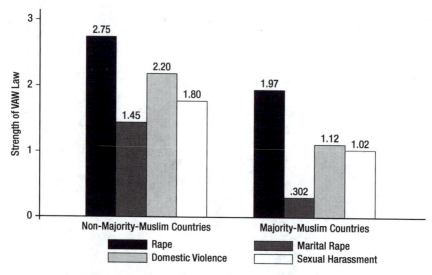

Figure 5.7   Average legal strength scores by majority-Muslim status, 2007–2010.

in the lower half. So, even among majority-Muslim subregions, Western Asia is much less likely than others to have legal protections of any kind.[3]

In more-sophisticated analyses that follow later in this chapter, we return to the question of religion's possible role on the adoption of laws offering protections against gender-based violence. These further analyses will allow us to examine the interplay of majority religion and other country-specific factors in how they affect the adoption of gender-violence laws and how these laws affect outcomes such as women's status.

Form of Political Organization

One might wager that a federal state should have lower scores on our legal indicators, since the sovereignty of subnational political units might lead to a patchwork of uneven laws. The counterargument would be that while federal states can (and do) have uneven laws in many respects, there are also large threads of consistency, typically brought on by federal leadership in an issue area. That thread of consistency, however, need not necessarily be empowering to women in all states. Our data allow us to examine such propositions, and we find that unitary states have slightly better rape laws than do federal states (means of 2.72 and 2.54, respectively, a statistically significant difference). On the other hand, federal states have better sexual harassment laws (means of 1.82 and 1.57, respectively, a statistically significant difference). The differences between federal and unitary states regarding marital-rape and domestic violence laws are not statistically significant, meaning any difference could be due to chance alone.

Commonality

Do laws addressing rape, marital rape, sexual harassment, and domestic violence have anything meaningful in common with one another in practice, or are they totally discrete components of countries' legal systems? Is there any pattern to the granting of these legal protections by states? Table 5.2 shows the result of a Mokken scale analysis of our legal guarantees data for 2007 and 2010 that helps answer these and other questions. We show the results for the first (2007) and last (2010) year of our data to demonstrate that they are extremely similar across time. The H statistic is the most important one in a Mokken scale analysis, indicating the overall strength of the scale. According to Mokken's (1971) rule, an H score between 0.3 and 0.4 constitutes a weak scale, between 0.4 and 0.5 demonstrates medium scalability, and an H score above 0.5 shows a strong scale.

With overall scale H scores of 0.51 and 0.50, we see that all four types of legal guarantees formed relatively strong cumulative scales in 2007 and 2010, respectively. From a measurement perspective, this means the H scores in Table 5.2 provide empirical corroboration for our assumption that all four of these indicators have something strongly in common with one another. Substantively, these scales tell us that these four types of laws do not act completely independent of one another. That is, what constitutes "the law" with regard to violence against women is a fabric of statutes rather than a collection of isolated statutes. Knowing that these laws have a strong commonality with one another underscores law-making as a historically cumulative process rather than a set of decisions made in isolation. These results may also suggest that those seeking to enhance laws on gender violence would do well to frame their appeals such that the overall aim is the enhancement of women's dignity rather than merely the enactment any specific statute. This not only provides a consistent frame for advocacy, but helps create a cohesive *body* of law and thereby sends strong cues to a society about the worth of females.

Table 5.2 Scaling Analysis Results

2007 N = 193 Scale Coefficient H = **0.51**		2010 N = 195 Scale Coefficient H = **0.50**	
Item	Item H	Item	Item H
Marital Rape	0.54	Marital Rape	0.54
Sexual Harassment	0.44	Sexual Harassment	0.42
Domestic Violence	0.55	Domestic Violence	0.54
Rape	0.51	Rape	0.48

Sequence

Beyond knowing these laws have something in common with one another, is there any kind of general sequence in which gender-violence laws are enacted? Is there a specific legal guarantee that countries regularly offer before or after all the others? Luckily, the analyses that produced the results in Table 5.2 satisfied a particular statistical test, so both scales can inform us about the sequence in which these laws reach full, explicit protection against these forms of violence.[4] The sequence of enactment—the order in which we would expect any given country to offer and fully enshrine these four legal guarantees—is, from first to last: rape, domestic violence, sexual harassment, and marital rape. This is identical to the ordering of the laws by their degree of strength (rape has the strongest legal guarantees, followed by domestic violence, and so forth), detailed in Figure 5.1.

One important takeaway from the fact that the sequence (order of adoption of laws) and hierarchy (order of the laws by degree of strength) are identical is that legal frameworks addressing violence against women tend to strengthen over time as protections for further forms of violence are added, rather than degrade under the weight of an expanding set of laws. This is important for a number of reasons. First, it says to policymakers and activists, "Don't wait to make perfect legal protections against one form of violence before advocating for protections addressing other forms, as these protections are mutually reinforcing." Advocates organized around different forms of violence should be encouraged to work together as much as possible. Second, the commonality of sequence and hierarchy implies that social learning is taking place in the direction of greater legal recourse for female victims of violence. Violence against women remains a troubling pandemic, certainly, but this is some good news.

Throughout this book we've invoked the now-common assertion that violence against women has been inadequately addressed as a human rights violation, as a matter of international law, or in either state domestic policy or practice because it occurs dominantly in the private realm of life rather than in the public realm. This assertion should be somewhat testable with our legal data. We begin by assuming different forms of violence against women are private and/or public to different extents. We would assert that sexual harassment is the most public form, followed by rape, domestic violence, and then marital rape as the most private form.

Figure 5.8 illustrates two hypotheses about the hierarchy and sequence of our four types of laws, based on this assumption of their relative public/private qualities. If our ordering of these forms of gender violence based on their public/private qualities were correct, and if this dimension (public/private attributes) were the key factor in explaining the absence/presence of laws protecting against these four forms of violence, we would expect to see two things illustrated in Figure 5.8. First, we would expect to see the greatest legal protection against sexual harassment, followed by rape, domestic violence, and then marital rape. In Figure 5.8, this is illustrated as the "hierarchy" thesis, set out to the left of the pyramid. The shading in the pyramid represents the hypothesized public/private nature of these forms of violence. Second, we would expect to see full respect for these four types of laws in any given country to be ordered as sexual harassment first, then rape, domestic violence, and, last, marital rape. In Figure 5.8 this is illustrated as the "sequence" thesis, set out to the right of the pyramid.

However, the scaling results from Table 5.2 make clear that the hypotheses illustrated in Figure 5.8 are not supported. Instead we find that, for example, the most public form of violence (sexual harassment) is the next-to-last to be fully legally protected. Legal protections against rape and domestic violence are also ordered/sequenced differently than we would expect if the public/private nature of these forms of violence were the dominant determinant of their adoption by countries. That said, we did find that marital rape, which we posited as being the most private of our four forms of violence against women, was also the last and least to be protected. Perhaps the public/private nature of a given form of gender violence is related to its legal address at the extremes. While not a perfect fit, rape was our second most public form of violence and was found to be most strongly protected against legally and the most likely to be fully protected in any given country.

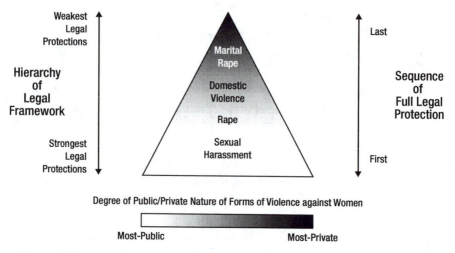

Figure 5.8   Hypothesized hierarchy and sequence of legal guarantees relating to violence against women, by public/private status.

If the public/private degree of a particular form of violence is not the driving force behind the ordering in Table 5.2, then what is? Perhaps legal guarantees against each of these forms of violence against women constitute threats to traditional (male-centric) societal structuring. Are laws barring marital rape a greater threat to traditional male privilege or male standing than are domestic violence laws? Perhaps sexual conquest over a spouse is seen as acceptable, whereas other forms of physical or mental abuse against intimate partners are not. Is spousal rape seen as legitimate sexual dominion of man over woman, whereas (regardless of its actual varieties of practice), domestic violence is seen as a less legitimate nonsexual dominion?

The Best and Worst

Because the analyses in Table 5.2 demonstrate that legal protections for our four forms of violence against women share strong commonalities, we were able to add each country's score on all four indicators to form an index of overall legal protections against VAW. The scale ranges from 0 (no legal protections for any of these four indicators) to 12 (full legal protections for all four indicators). It is important to remember that "full legal protections" does not mean "perfect legal protections." *All* countries could use improvement in their laws addressing *all four* of these types of violence. For example, the United States is on the "full protections" list. Recall, however, our discussion in Chapter 4 about how it could use improved laws protecting rape victims against harmful child-custody claims (among other things). "Full guarantees" here means the existence of legal protection from a form of violence meets the threshold of "acceptable and explicit" set out in the previous chapter.

Table 5.3 lists countries that, in 2010, evidenced full legal protections and those that evidenced none. As a baseline for comparison, in 2010 the average score, globally, was 7.48 (out of 12). There were more countries in 2010 with full protections than with no protections, and there is some meaningful regional diversity among countries with full protections. Six regions of the world—Africa, Asia, Oceania, Europe, Latin America, and North America—have countries with full legal protections.

Table 5.3 Overall Strength of Legal Protections for Four Forms of Violence against Women, 2010

FULL Legal Protections	NO Legal Protections
Australia	Democratic People's Republic of Korea
Austria	Jordan
Belgium	Lebanon
Chile	Maldives
Colombia	Mauritania
Costa Rica	Saudi Arabia
Croatia	Yemen
Germany	
Greece	
Israel	
Moldova	
Monaco	
Namibia	
New Zealand	
Poland	
San Marino	
Sao Tome and Principe	
Serbia	
Slovakia	
Sweden	
Switzerland	
United Kingdom	
United States	

Figure 5.9 shows the geospatial distribution of our index of overall legal protections. All seven countries with no legal protections for any of the four types of violence against women are found within the Asian region (see the large patch of lightly shaded countries on the map). Looking at the subregional level, we see that five of these seven countries (71 percent) are in Western Asia. Thus, there is great geospatial concentration among countries with the worst records on gender-violence laws. Indeed, a full 60 percent of the countries scoring below a 4 are in the Asian region. This firmly reinforces the story about Western Asia we discussed with reference to Table 5.1.

What Factors Explain the Strength of VAW Legal Guarantees?

To empirically test the hypotheses presented earlier in the book, we ran a series of statistical analyses enabling us to determine whether a relationship exists between the social, political, and economic factors introduced by our hypotheses in Chapters 2 and 3, and the strength of legal guarantees protecting women from violence. We also conducted a number of such analyses assessing the relationship between the strength of legal guarantees and several well-known indicators of women's status/outcomes. Here we share our findings.

Testable Hypotheses

A hypothesis is a statement about the relationship between two variables. Hypotheses are generated by expectations rooted in theory. Theoretical expectations are proposed answers to research questions. For example, our primary research question is *What factors explain the strength of VAW legal guarantees?* One answer involves women's political participation and the role of female policymakers representing women's issues in government (see Chapter 2). The *answer* is rooted in extant theory regarding the role of female representatives in government. From this theory, we can generate a testable hypothesis. A testable hypothesis states the direction of the relationship we expect to observe between the two variables if our theory is correct (King, Keohane, and Verba 1994). For example, a hypothesis generated from the women's political participation theory is *Countries with higher levels of women's political participation are more likely than others to adopt legal guarantees protecting women from violence.* If we find that the relationship between the two variables holds in our analysis, we have provided evidence for our theory. The hypotheses examined in this book are stated at the end of Chapters 2 and 3.

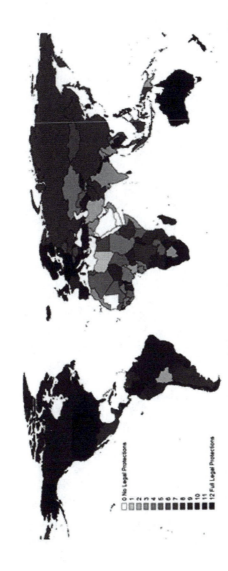

Figure 5.9 Index of overall legal protections against four forms of violence against women, 2010.

To examine the influence of various factors on the strength of VAW legal guarantees, our primary dependent variable of interest is the strength of legal protections related to VAW. We utilize our original indicators of the strength of domestic legal protections against rape, marital rape, domestic violence, and sexual harassment. These are the same indicators whose construction we described in Chapter 4. In addition to explaining the various factors associated with the strength of VAW legal protections, we are interested in the influence of the strength of legal protections on women's status. As a result, we use various indicators of women's status/outcomes as dependent variables in additional analyses. These variables are described in detail in Appendix B.

To determine the factors that are associated with (or explain) the strength of legal guarantees, we also utilize several independent variables in our analysis. The variables examined capture political, economic, cultural, societal, and international factors we argued to be associated with the strength of VAW legal protections. Appendix B contains full list of these variables.

Variables
Variables are the elements of our hypotheses that vary or change. In a statistical analysis, the dependent variable is the variable whose quantity or quality one is seeking to explain. An independent variable (explanatory variable) is an indicator that seeks to explain the level of, or changes in, the dependent variable. For example, in the hypothesis *Countries with higher levels of women's political participation are more likely than others to adopt legal guarantees protecting women from violence*, the dependent variable is the adoption of legal guarantees protecting women from violence and the independent variable is women's political participation. Appendix B contains a full list of the dependent and independent variables used in our analyses.

What Domestic and International Factors Matter?

Table 5.4 presents results from models examining the relationship between various independent variables and the strength of legal protections against rape, spousal rape, domestic violence, and sexual harassment, as well as the enforcement of legal guarantees. Table 5.4 indicates that religious institutions, women's political participation, women's economic rights, women's economic empowerment, international law, and trade all show a statistically significant relationship with the strength of various VAW legal protections, as well as enforcement of those protections.

Statistical Significance

What do the values in Tables 5.4 and 5.5 mean? At the bottom of the table, N indicates the number of observations (country-years) included in the estimation of each model. The *prob > chi²* indicates whether we can reject the null hypothesis, which states that the independent variables in the models have no influence on the dependent variable they are trying to explain. A small p-value (i.e., < 0.0001) indicates that we can be confident in rejecting the null hypothesis that all of the coefficients in the model are zero—that is, we can conclude that the independent variables in the models better explain the dependent variables than if we had examined models without these independent variables.

We are particularly interested in whether our results are reliable, or statistically significant. Reliable results indicate that we are confident the relationship between an independent variable and a dependent variable (legal-protection strength) is not entirely due to chance. We are also interested in the direction of any relationship, positive or negative. For example, a positive relationship might be one where, as respect for women's economic rights increase, there is a corresponding positive increase in legal protections. That is, as one factor increases, the other increases. In a negative relationship, however, as one factor increases, the other decreases. To determine reliability, we use a p-value threshold of 0.10, which indicates that we want to be at least 90 percent certain that the relationship between the two variables is not due to chance. We consider variables for which we cannot achieve that level of certainty to be unreliable. In our tables, the letters *P, p, N,* and *n* represent whether the relationship between an independent variable and a dependent variable is positive (**P,** p) or negative (**N,** n); boldfaced capitalization indicates whether that relationship is statistically reliable (**P, N**) or statistically unreliable (p, n).

Figure 5.10 indicates the relationship of each statistically reliable variable and the adoption of full legal protections against each form of violence. More specifically, the figure indicates the probability of a state adopting full legal protections against each form of violence, given specific changes in the independent variables.

Reading a Probability Bar Chart

How does one interpret the results presented in Figure 5.10? Based on Figure 5.10, we can talk about more than the fact that there is a relationship between two things; we can talk about the extent or size of a relationship. Specifically, the bars in Figure 5.10 represent the change in the probability that a country adopts a full legal protection against rape, marital rape, and so on (a score of 3), given a one-standard-deviation increase in the value of a given variable, taking into account all the other variables in each model in Table 5.4 (other variables are set to either their mode or median). For variables that only take on two values (i.e., the majority-Muslim variable can take on a value of 1, meaning countries are majority Muslim, or 0, meaning countries are not majority Muslim), the bars in Figure 5.10 represent the change in probability of adopting a full legal protection for country-years where the variable is equal to 0 (i.e., non–majority Muslim) as compared to country-years where the variable is equal to 1 (i.e., majority Muslim), taking into account all the other variables in the model.

In other words, the bar represents the *difference* in the probability of adopting full legal protections between a country that is non–majority Muslim and a country that is majority Muslim. Bars extending to the right of the vertical line at zero represent higher probabilities of adopting full legal protections. Bars extending to the left of the vertical line at zero represent lower probabilities of adopting full legal protections.

Women's Political Participation

What role does women's political participation have on the strength of legal protections related to violence against women? Table 5.4 shows that women's political participation has a positive and reliable relationship with the strength of protections related to marital rape, domestic violence, sexual harassment, and total legal guarantees. Figure 5.10 shows that as the percentage of women in a national legislature increases by about 10 percent (one standard deviation from the median), countries are about 10 percent more likely to adopt full legal protection against marital rape, domestic violence, and sexual harassment. Further, as the percentage of women in the national legislature increases by about 10 percent, countries are about 13 percent more likely to score in the upper quartile on total laws, or a 10–12 on the total laws variable. We report changes in the probability of being in the upper quartile (10–12) on the total laws variable (rather than a 12 on total laws) because the probability of being in any single category of the total laws variable (including 12) is low, given that the variable ranges 0–12, rather than 0–3 like the individual legal protections variables. Consequently, the upper quartile provides a better representation of outcomes we would expect to observe.

As an example of this relationship, in 2009 Azerbaijan's parliament was composed of 11.4 percent women (14 women held seats in a 123-seat parliament). In 2009 Azerbaijan scored a 1 on domestic violence legal protections, indicating that the law was incomplete. However, in 2010 Azerbaijan's parliament was composed of 16 percent women (20 women held seats in a 125-seat parliament).

Table 5.4 Influence of Independent Variables on Legal Protections against VAW (Stereotype Logistic Regression Results)

	Rape	Marital Rape	Domestic Violence	Sexual Harassment	Total Laws	Enforcement
Societal Discrimination	p	p	p	p	p	**P**
Majority Muslim	**N**	**N**	n	**N**	**N**	**N**
Majority Christian	**N**	n	p	n	p	**N**
Contiguity	—	p	p	**P**	p	**P**
CEDAW Ratification Years	**N**	n	**P**	n	n	p
CEDAW Reservation (Art. 2)	p	**N**	**N**	p	np	
Women in Legislature	p	**P**	**P**	**P**	**P**	p
Trafficking Law	—	**P**	**P**	**P**	**P**	p
Women's Economic Rights	**P**	**P**	p	p	p	**P**
Fertility Rate	**N**	n	**N**	n	n	n
Empowerment Rights	**P**	**P**	**P**	**N**	**P**	p
GNI (logged)	**N**	p	n	p	p	p
Trade	n	n	p	**N**	**N**	p
Total VAW Laws	—	—	—	—	—	**P**
Civil War	—	—	—	—	—	**N**
N	704	703	703	703	703	703
P > chi²	0.010	0.000	0.000	0.000	0.000	0.000

P = Statistically reliable positive relationship
p = Statistically unreliable positive relationship
N = Statistically reliable negative relationship
n = Statistically unreliable negative relationship

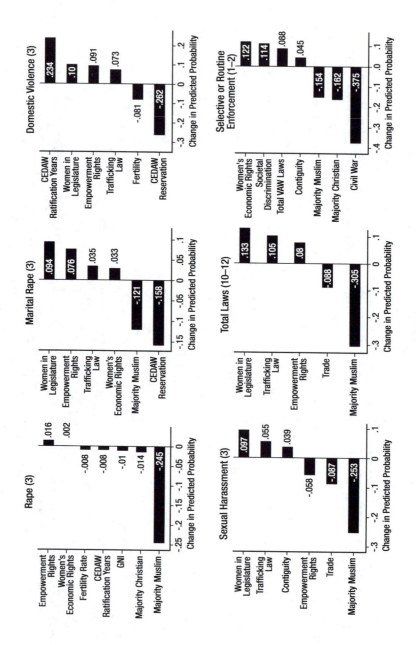

Figure 5.10 Probability of adopting full legal protection.

In 2010 Azerbaijan scored a 3 on domestic violence legal protections, namely because new legislation was passed making domestic violence a criminal offense and establishing shelters for victims. Notably, Mehriban Aliyeva, the first lady of the Republic of Azerbaijan and a member of parliament, was an active lobbyist for the law (Gureyeva 2012).

This is a fascinating and robust finding, as much has been made in the comparative development literature of the fact that women in a national legislature are likely not representative of women writ large in a country because they come from elite families, are not feminists (because feminists are filtered out by nomination processes), and are token representatives without real power to affect an agenda, among other things (Beteta 2006). Our finding, however, provides evidence that women in government may indeed be representative of women's interests in the realm of laws addressing gender violence. This provides a connection between comparative work, where this factor is used uneasily, and American politics scholarship, where there is an enduring understanding that female legislators represent female interests in their legislation (Reingold 2008).

Women's Economic Rights

Turning to women's economic rights, Table 5.4 shows that women's economic rights have a positive and reliable relationship with the strength of rape and marital-rape legal protections as well as enforcement of legal protections. More specifically, a one-point increase (one standard deviation) in the CIRI index of women's economic rights is associated with a 0.2 percent increase in the probability of adopting full rape legal protections and a 3.3 percent increase in the probability of adopting full marital-rape legal protections. These increases are relatively small in magnitude, however, particularly when compared with the finding that the same increase in women's economic rights is associated with a 12.2 percent increase in the probability of a country engaging in selective or routine enforcement (scoring a 1 or 2 on enforcement) of VAW legal protections.

This finding is interesting because when women possess greater economic decision-making power, law-enforcement personnel appear to more easily enforce VAW legal protections. Greater economic rights and increased access to resources create greater opportunities for women to escape violent situations in the private sphere (at home), as well as in the public sphere. This pattern is observed in Angola, which scored a 0 on women's economic rights in 2008, indicating that there were no economic rights for women in society that year. In the same year

Angola received a 0 for enforcement of VAW legal protections. In 2009 Angola scored a 1 on women's economic rights, indicating some economic rights were in place for women (rights such as equal pay for equal work, equality in hiring practices, and the like). Along with an improvement in economic rights in 2009 came a corresponding improvement in the enforcement of VAW legal protections. Angola scored a 1 on enforcement in 2009, indicating selective enforcement of VAW legal protections.

Women's Economic Empowerment

Women's economic empowerment is reliably associated with the strength of rape and domestic violence legal protections. For our analyses, we used fertility rate as a proxy for women's economic empowerment. Figure 5.10 shows that an increase in total fertility rate of 1.5 children (one standard deviation) is associated with a 0.8 percent decrease in the probability of adopting full rape legal protections and an 8.1 percent decrease in the probability of adopting full domestic violence legal protections. That the effect is much greater with respect to domestic violence indicates that women in larger families or women with more children find it relatively more difficult to escape situations of violence and may experience greater isolation from the public or formal economic sphere, making them less able to mobilize around the passage of stronger domestic violence legislation. Rwanda illustrates this relationship: in 2007 it had a fertility rate of 5.167 and scored a 0 on domestic violence legal protections. However, in 2010 Rwanda's fertility rate had declined to 4.841 and the country scored a 2 on domestic violence legal protections.

Economic Globalization

Looking at economic globalization, we find that trade is negatively and reliably associated with the strength of sexual harassment and total VAW legal protections. In other words, as the sum of trade in merchandise as a percent of GDP increases by about 35 percent (one standard deviation), the strength of sexual harassment and total VAW legal protections (all four legal protections) decreases. We find that an increase of around 35 percentage points (one standard deviation) in the sum of trade in merchandise as a percent of GDP is associated with around an 8.7 percent decrease in the probability of adopting full legal guarantees against sexual harassment and an 8.8 percent decrease in the probability of being in the upper quartile of the total laws variable (scoring a 10–12). Given that sexual harassment legal protections are often enforced in the workplace, perhaps trade liberalization encourages some kind of "race to the bottom" (as posited in Chapter 2) where governments avoid involvement in the private economic sphere. Consider, as an example, the case of Jamaica in 2008, which had trade in merchandise around 79.7 percent of GDP (above the mean of around 70 percent). Jamaica scored a 0 on sexual harassment legal protections in 2008. The country's trade orientation has focused extensively on developing its textile-, apparel-, and garment-manufacturing industries. Significant discrimination in employment plagues the Jamaican economy, in which most unemployed professionals and unpaid workers are women (Tindigarukayo 2006). Competition among women for employment leads to significant discrimination in employment and women remain vulnerable to sexual harassment and are afraid to report cases. Further, due to an absence of legislation, no comprehensive policy exists in cases of sexual harassment, and many places of employment have no policy on sexual harassment. The isolated nature of much female employment in Jamaica likely also deters mobilization around the adoption of legislation (95).

Societal Discrimination

Our indicator of societal discrimination is positively and reliably associated with the *enforcement* of VAW-related legal protections. In other words, improvements in societal discrimination or relatively lower levels of societal discrimination are associated with higher levels of VAW-related law enforcement. More specifically, a one-point improvement in societal discrimination (i.e., from high societal discrimination to some societal discrimination) is associated with an 11.4 percent increase in the probability of a country having selective or routine enforcement of VAW-related legal protections. Given that high levels of societal discrimination are often a result of the underreporting or fear of reporting rooted in cultural or societal factors, it is likely that where women fear reporting violence, law-enforcement personnel are significantly inhibited in their ability to perform their jobs.

Religious Institutions

With respect to religion, we find that majority-Muslim countries are negatively and reliably associated with the strength of legal guarantees related to rape, spousal rape, sexual harassment, total VAW-related legal protections, and enforcement of

VAW-related legal protections. In other words, even accounting for all the factors in our model set out in Table 5.4, majority-Muslim countries are still less likely to adopt strong legal protections and enforce those legal protections than are non-majority-Muslim countries. We find that majority-Muslim countries have a 24.5 percent lower probability of adopting a strong rape legal protection, a 12.1 percent lower probability of adopting full marital-rape legal protections, and a 25.3 percent lower probability of adopting full sexual harassment legal protections than non-majority-Muslim countries. Further, majority-Muslim countries have a 30.5 percent lower probability of scoring in the top quartile of total legal protections (10–12 on total laws) and a 15.4 percent lower probability of selectively or routinely enforcing VAW-related legal protections than non-majority-Muslim countries.

We find that majority-Christian countries are relatively less likely to adopt full legal protections against rape and to selectively and routinely enforce VAW-related legal protections. More specifically, majority-Christian countries have a 1.4 percent lower probability of adopting full rape laws and a 16.2 percent lower probability of enforcing VAW-legal protections than non-majority-Christian countries. Our findings support the notion that many religious institutions place women in a subordinate position and may inhibit women's ability to mobilize around policy-related issues. Further, where these legal protections have been established, religious institutions may play a role in the ability of law-enforcement personnel to enforce legislation. Consider the case of Iraq in 2010, in which the US State Department indicates, "Local NGOs and media reporting indicated that domestic violence often went unreported and unpunished with abuses customarily addressed within the family and tribal structure. Harassment of legal personnel working on domestic violence cases, as well as a lack of police and judicial personnel, further hampered efforts to bring perpetrators to justice" (US Department of State 2010b). The stigma attached to the enforcement of legal guarantees where religious institutions play a major role in society appears to obstruct the law enforcement's ability to carry out their tasks.

International Law and the Strength of Women's Movements

The number of years for which a country has been party to the Convention on the Elimination of All Forms of Discrimination against Women (CEDAW) has a reliable and negative relationship with the strength of rape legal protections, and a reliable and positive relationship with the strength of domestic violence legal protections. That is, as the time since a country has ratified CEDAW increases by about eight years, a country is 0.8 percent less likely to have strong legal protections against rape and 23.4 percent more likely to have strong domestic violence legal protections. Given that the average global strength of rape legal protections is particularly high (Figure 5.1) and rape legal protections are typically guaranteed earlier in the sequence of legal protections (Table 5.2), the ratification of CEDAW likely has little marginal utility on the strength of rape laws as time passes, which may explain the negative and substantively small finding. With respect to domestic violence, however, the finding is substantively meaningful and consistent with the sequencing shown in Table 5.2. That is, most countries have adopted strong legal protections against rape, indicating that it is widely deemed unacceptable by society. We find that domestic violence is typically ordered as the next legal guarantee to be adopted, followed by sexual harassment and marital rape. Following the ratification of CEDAW, women's-rights policy likely cascades in the domestic legal system, where countries first adopt strong rape legal protections (if they were not already in existence) and then strong domestic violence legal protections. Perhaps on average states have adopted strong legal protections against rape but are still in the process of establishing domestic violence policy nationally. In 1992 the Committee on the Elimination of Discrimination against Women adopted General Recommendation 19, which specifically addresses domestic violence policy, including the necessity of criminal penalties for perpetrators and rehabilitation programs for victims.

In addition, we find that resistance to international law has a negative and reliable relationship with the strength of marital-rape and domestic violence legal protections. In fact, countries that hold a reservation to Article 2 of CEDAW are 15.8 percent less likely to adopt full marital-rape legal protections and 26.2 percent less likely to adopt full domestic violence legal protections. These findings are substantively meaningful and provide interesting insights, particularly with respect to marital rape. CEDAW ratification alone has little influence on the strength of marital-rape legal protections; however, resistance to CEDAW, as evidenced through the placement of reservations to the treaty, has a profound negative influence on the strength of marital-rape protections.

Regional Diffusion

Turning to our regional diffusion hypothesis, we find that the mean sexual harassment legal protections for all contiguous countries has a positive and reliable relationship with the strength of sexual harassment legal protections, and the mean enforcement of VAW legal protections for all contiguous countries has a positive relationship with a country's enforcement of VAW legal protections. More specifically, as sexual harassment legal protections for contiguous countries increases by about 0.5 points (one standard deviation), a country is 3.9 percent more likely to adopt strong legal protections against sexual harassment. Further, as the mean enforcement of VAW legal protections increases by about 0.5 points (one standard deviation), a country is 4.5 percent more likely to have selective or routine enforcement of those protections. Perhaps because sexual harassment largely occurs in the public sphere, policies lend themselves to imitation by other countries. As economic growth occurs in states within different regions and more women enter the workforce, states begin to consider adopting sexual harassment legislation and look to their neighbors who may be experiencing similar economic-growth patterns and similar patterns of women entering the workforce.

Civil War

We find that civil war has a negative and reliable relationship with enforcement. More specifically, countries experiencing civil war are 37.5 percent less likely to engage in selective or routine enforcement of legal protections related to VAW. Whether violence against women is used as a weapon of war, making it widespread and difficult to enforce, or whether enforcement is problematic because of the breakdown of domestic institutions and the inherent political instability associated with internal conflict, civil war is a powerful predictor of the enforcement of VAW policy and contributes significantly to the failure of law-enforcement personnel to enforce VAW-related legislation.

Legal Guarantees and Enforcement

Is the strength of legal guarantees related to the enforcement of VAW legal protections? This question highlights whether the influence of strong legal protections is more than just a parchment barrier to VAW. That is, it highlights whether legislation goes beyond simple codification and recognition in law, and asks whether legal protections are influential in practice. We find that the strength of VAW legal protections has a reliable and positive relationship with the enforcement of those protections. That is, as the total VAW legal protections in a country increase by about three points (or a country adopts an additional full legal protection against one form of VAW), the country is 8.8 percent more likely to selectively or routinely enforce VAW-related legislation. As VAW-related policy begins to cascade throughout society, perhaps members of society begin to view VAW as increasingly socially unacceptable and, in turn, law-enforcement personnel face less resistance in carrying out the law.

Alternative Explanations

Turning to some of the variables in the models accounting for alternative explanations of VAW-related laws, we find that empowerment rights have a positive and reliable relationship with rape, marital rape, and domestic violence legal protections, as well as total legal protections. More specifically, as empowerment rights increase by about four points (one standard deviation), the probability of adopting full rape, marital-rape, and domestic violence legal protections increases by 1.6 percent, 7.6 percent, and 9.1 percent, respectively. Consider, for example, the case of Uganda, which in 2008 scored a 1 on the empowerment rights index, indicating almost a complete lack of empowerment rights. Also in 2008, Uganda scored a 1 on domestic violence legislation, indicating that the legislation was incomplete. However, in 2010 Uganda scored a 4 on empowerment rights, with a notable improvement in the electoral self-determination score. More specifically, the country moved from a lack of self-determination through free and fair elections (score of 0) to a limited right to electoral self-determination in practice (score of 1). Along with an increase in empowerment rights, Uganda saw a corresponding improvement in the strength of domestic violence legislation. In 2010, it passed legislation that criminalized domestic violence, expanded protections for victims, and instituted penalties for perpetrators.

Interestingly, empowerment rights have a negative and reliable relationship with the strength of sexual harassment legal protections. In fact, as empowerment rights increase by around four points, the probability of having full sexual harassment legal protections decreases by 5.8 percent. Democracies, or states that generally have greater empowerment rights, often place a relatively greater emphasis on the free market (the lack of government regulation in the marketplace). Given that sexual harassment legislation involves regulation of the marketplace to some degree, perhaps states with more empowerment rights experience greater resistance to this type of regulation.

Exploring Women's Outcomes

Table 5.5 shows the influence of total VAW legal protections on gender inequality, human development, and women's HIV rates (and can be read in the same way as Table 5.4).

Reading Figure 5.11

Figure 5.11 presents substantive results for all statistically reliable variables in the models. The values presented in the figure represent standardized regression coefficients, which show the influence of a one-standard-deviation change of the independent variable on the standard-deviation change in the dependent variable. By standardizing the regression coefficients, we can directly compare the regression coefficients of the independent variables with one another. Bars extending to the right of the zero line indicate a positive relationship between the independent variable and each of the dependent variables: gender inequality (higher levels of inequality), human development, and women's HIV rates. Bars extending to the left of the zero line indicate a negative relationship between each of the independent variables and the dependent variables, gender inequality (lower levels of inequality or greater equality), human development, and women's HIV rates.

Table 5.5 Influence of VAW Legal Protections on Women's Outcomes (Regression Results)

	GII	HDI	Female HIV Rate
Total VAW Laws	N	P	N
Societal Discrimination	N	P	P
Majority Muslim	P	p	n
Majority Christian	P	p	P
Contiguity	n	P	N
CEDAW Ratification Years	N	n	N
CEDAW Reservation (Art. 2)	p	n	N
Empowerment Rights	n	n	n
GNI (logged)	N	—	N
Trade	N	P	p
Civil War	p	N	n
Women in Legislature	—	N	N
Women's Economic Rights	—	P	N
N	135	487	454
R^2	0.7545	0.5313	0.4811

P = Statistically reliable positive relationship
p = Statistically unreliable positive relationship
N = Statistically reliable negative relationship
n = Statistically unreliable negative relationship

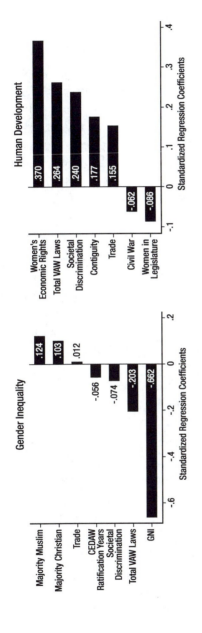

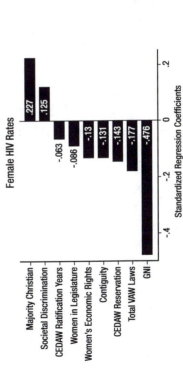

Figure 5.11 Influence of VAW laws on women's outcomes (stereotype logistic regression results).

The primary variable of interest, total VAW legal protections, has a negative relationship with gender inequality. The results indicate that a 1-standard-deviation increase in the strength of VAW legal protections (an increase of around 3 on a scale ranging 0–12) is associated with a 0.203 standard-deviation decrease in gender inequality, or a 0.04-point decrease in gender inequality (ranging 0–1). Figure 5.11 also shows that strengthening VAW legal protections is about twice as effective as decreasing VAW-related societal discrimination and almost three times more effective than CEDAW ratification. The only variable that has a stronger relationship with gender inequality is gross national income (GNI). It appears that, on average, as more women enter the formal workforce, women are generating higher levels of income, and a rise in income is associated with greater equality in our model.

VAW legal protections also are associated with relatively higher levels of human development. Figure 5.11 shows that a 1-standard-deviation increase in VAW-related legal protections (about three points, or one full legal protection) is associated with a 0.264-standard-deviation increase in human development, or around a 0.05-point increase in the human-development index, which is substantial on a scale ranging 0–1. VAW-related societal discrimination is a good predictor of human development, as well. The only variable in the model that has a stronger relationship with human development is women's economic rights, which is associated with a 0.37-standard-deviation increase, or a 0.07-point increase, in human development. VAW-related societal discrimination is a good predictor of human development as well. A 1-standard-deviation increase in VAW-related societal discrimination (a one-unit increase in the variable, in which higher values represent relatively lower levels of societal discrimination) is associated with a 0.24-standard-deviation increase in human development, or a 0.04-point increase in the human-development index.

Finally, Table 5.5 shows that the strength of VAW legal protections has a negative and reliable relationship with the percentage of women living with HIV (out of all persons living with HIV in the country). A 1-standard-deviation increase in the strength of VAW-related legal protections (about three points, or one full legal protection) is associated with a 0.177-standard-deviation decrease (2.5 percent) in the number of women living with HIV out of all persons living with HIV. Figure 5.11 shows that a 1-standard-deviation increase in societal discrimination (around a one-point increase, which indicates lower levels of societal discrimination) is associated with a 0.125-standard-deviation (1.78 percent) increase in female HIV rates.

Perhaps in countries with lower levels of societal discrimination, women have fewer fears of societal reprisal when they seek medical attention for HIV or report that violence against them led to medical problems. As a result, levels of reporting may be higher in countries with relatively lower levels of societal discrimination. The only variables exhibiting stronger relationships with female HIV rates than VAW legal protections are GNI and majority-Christian status, indicating that as income rises, female HIV rates drop significantly and majority-Christian countries have higher female HIV rates than non-majority-Christian countries. These findings provide evidence that the strength of legal protections related to VAW reduces societal costs associated with women's health problems.

In these analyses the strength of legal protections against VAW is found to be reliably associated with various indicators of women's outcomes. While no reliable or consistent cross-national data exist on women's outcomes directly related to VAW, these outcomes indicators provide initial evidence of the role that strong legal protections against VAW play in reducing levels of VAW worldwide.

Conclusion

Several findings presented in this chapter are notable. We find legal protections against rape to be the strongest of the four types examined, and those against marital rape to be the weakest. However, on a global scale all forms of VAW would benefit from legal reform. In examining the various regions of the world, we find Asia, particularly Western Asia, to offer the weakest legal protections against all forms of VAW, suggesting substantial need for policy reform. We also find that legal protections are related to one another, and gender-based-violence legal protections are not solely a collection of isolated statutes. Legal protections against rape and domestic violence tend to emerge earlier in the sequence of enacting these laws, while sexual harassment and marital-rape guarantees come later. This finding is substantively interesting, as the sequence or order of legal protections conflicts somewhat with the public/private nature of these types of VAW. Finally, we find that women's involvement is important in the strength of VAW legal protections. Specifically, the political participation, economic rights, and economic empowerment of women in a given country are all important in the adoption and strength of VAW legal guarantees. We find other factors—including international law and trade—are also important for the establishment and strength of VAW legal protections.

CONCLUSION

This is the conclusion to our book, but we hope it is the start to a new part of the discussion about law's ability to protect women from senseless violence. Here we outline several general conclusions from our study that we hope can add to such a discussion.[1] We also make some recommendations for further nourishing our understanding of the role law plays and, more importantly, *can play* in reducing violence against women (VAW).

First, in too many countries legal protections against gender violence have a long way to go toward being acceptable in any meaningful sense. Some countries have essentially no legal protection for women against violence, and some even sanction VAW. On the other end of the spectrum is a group of countries that have what we consider full legal guarantees. However, we are careful to note that "full guarantees" does not mean "perfect guarantees." All states can make improvements to their gender violence–related legal frameworks, and there seems to be no geographical barrier to achievement in this regard: six regions of the world were represented in our list of countries having full legal protections against rape, marital rape, domestic violence, and sexual harassment.

Second, domestic law matters. Simply because a country with gender-violence laws still experiences violence against women does not mean such laws are a bad idea or offer no protection. We find, for example, that countries with greater domestic legal protections against gender violence have less gender-based inequality, greater levels of human development, and lower female HIV rates, even when simultaneously accounting for a host of other possibilities that could affect these outcomes. Unlike law, not one of these alternative explanations was found to be associated with improvements in all three outcomes in our study: inequality, human development, and reduction of female HIV incidence.

Third, international law matters. The greater the number of years a country has been a party to CEDAW, the lower the gender inequality, female HIV rates, and the greater legal protections against domestic violence we can reliably expect that country to have. This opens the door for further research into the ways in which this happens. For example, based on Simmons's (2009) finding that social groups related to women's issues grow in number after CEDAW ratification, we left open the possibility that CEDAW ratification might indirectly prompt stronger laws through greater social mobilization. On the flip side, countries that have reserved out of CEDAW's Article 2—the centerpiece of the treaty—have weaker marital-rape and domestic violence laws.

Fourth, women's involvement matters in the effort to create laws protecting women. Countries with greater percentages of women in their national legislatures have stronger marital rape, domestic violence, and sexual harassment laws. Further, such countries are likely to have lower female HIV rates. This demonstrates that the longstanding finding from studies of United States politics—"women legislate on behalf of women"—also holds true internationally, at the very least in the issue area of violence against women. This provides some support for the inclusion of women's parliamentary representation in global indicators such as the United Nations Gender Inequality Index, and implies that efforts to make national legislatures more gender-inclusive, perhaps through the use of parliamentary electoral quotas for women, might be a fruitful avenue for addressing the structural foundations of violence against women.

Fifth, the classic dichotomy of the public and private spheres of women's lives may be more useful as a heuristic than as an actual guideline to understanding the adoption and/or status of domestic legal frameworks protecting women from violence. If feminist legal scholars are correct that the public-private dichotomy explains the adoption of laws relating to women in particular, then the aspects of women's lives addressed by these laws should be able to be ordered from most public to most private, and compared with the actual sequence of adoption (and strengthening toward full protection) of these laws. However, what we believed to be an intuitively reasonable ordering of our four types of violence against women from public to private did not correspond with the sequence of adoption of gender-violence laws returned by our scaling analyses. Only at the extreme was there a match in the hypothesized and the empirical orderings: we considered marital rape to be the most private of our forms of violence, and it was indeed the last in our sequence of laws. Reasons other than the purely private nature of the act may underlie this situation, however—for example, larger dynamics placing traditional social institutions such as marriage itself above the rights of any particular women may hinder passage of marital-rape laws. In one instance, a brief prepared by Ireland's Department of Justice for its minister of justice in advance of the legislative debate on what would become the Criminal Law (Rape) Act, 1981, included a minority report finding from the UK's Criminal Law Revision Committee (charged with making a recommendation on the institution of a marital-rape law) that noted if marital rape was made illegal and police involved, it could be detrimental to any reconciliation and fatally destructive to the family unit (Gartland 2011).

Sixth, domestic laws matter to one another. What constitutes "the law" with regard to violence against women is a fabric of statutes rather than a collection of isolated statutes. That is, laws are mutually reinforcing. Legal frameworks addressing violence against women tend to strengthen as new protections are added, not degrade under the weight of an expanding set of laws. Relatedly, we found that while unitary states may have more cohesive bodies of law than do federal states, this cohesion need not necessarily be more protective against gender violence. We found that while unitary states have marginally stronger rape laws, federal states have better sexual harassment laws. We found no reliable difference between the two forms of political organization with regard to their marital-rape or domestic violence laws.

Seventh, religion matters. Something about majority-Muslim countries, even ac-counting for many other possible factors, makes them significantly unequal and averse to implementing VAW laws. Majority-Muslim status was reliably associated with a reduced probability of having rape, marital-rape, and sexual harassment laws. Not only that, but simply being a majority-Muslim country was, by a great deal, the greatest inhibiting factor toward adoption of satisfactory rape and sexual harassment laws. For marital rape, majority-Muslim status was second only to a country's having reserved out of CEDAW's Article 2 in inhibiting laws ad-dressing this form of violence. Further, nearly 70 percent of countries with this reservation had a Muslim majority. Countries with a Christian majority were slightly more likely than those with a Muslim majority to impede enforcement of gender-violence laws. Majority-Christian status was also reliably associated with greater gender inequality and greater female HIV rates.

Eighth, what is it about Western Asia? Western Asia was, by far, the single subregion most responsible for Asia having the weakest legal protections against rape, marital rape, and domestic violence. Western Asia accounted for 44 percent of all countries, globally, receiving a 0, the lowest possible score, for rape laws in 2010; this despite Western Asia comprising only 10 percent of the countries in our sample. It does not appear to be the region's nearly universal majority-Muslim status, as many regions similar in this regard have greater legal protections. After investigating some other legal frameworks, our guess ended up being that Western Asian countries are less likely to offer their citizens legal protections of *any* kind, not just against gender violence. Certainly, this points to a need for case-based analysis of the countries in this region with regards to law and citizens' recourse to law.

Ninth, there is a sore need for systematic, comparative information about laws addressing violence against women. When we began our project of addressing the question of "How good are they?" about national laws on gender violence, we—perhaps naively—did not realize our efforts would be hampered by a lack of information about *what the laws are.* No comprehensive, cross-national, updated compendium of such laws exists. It is crucial, for the work of both policymakers and scholars, to have access to the text of current laws in legal systems so the difficulties and achievements of these legal formulations can be studied. Further, it is important to collect this information over time, as changes to laws are supposed to be improvements, and there is no way to know whether this is the case except with systematic documentation of change. Language barriers are an issue in creating and maintaining a collection of up-to-date gender-violence statutes, but (a) these are only small portions of a country's entire legal codes, (b) changes usually involve small amounts of text, and (c) local nongovernmental organizations' cooperation could help monitor changes in a country's code.

Tenth, even countries rated most highly in our data have room for legal improvements, and antiviolence activists must remain vigilant to protect extant legal protections from degradation. We use the case of the United States to illustrate this. In Table 5.3 the United States is listed among countries with full legal protections for our four forms of VAW. However, despite abundant statistics showing otherwise, denial of the pandemic that is violence against women is not uncommon in the United States. The disbelief that gender-based violence is a pandemic, or cynical political manipulation of the fact that it is, may help explain the shocking disparity in how violence against women is treated relative to other crimes in the United States. And there is indeed quite a disparity:

According to Human Rights Watch, the arrest rate in 2010 for accused rapists in the U.S. was 24%, the exact same rate as in 1970. Meanwhile, according to a CBS investigative report, 79% of murder suspects and 51% of those suspected of committing aggravated assault are arrested. (Bachman 2012)

One US critic of both sexual discrimination–related feminist jurisprudence and the school of thought known as dominance feminism has stated that widespread societal acceptance of the feminist claim of "a large number of unreported and unknown cases of sexual abuse" would ultimately unleash a web of "otherwise unthinkable" laws such as the legal abolishment of the nuclear family (Greer 2000, 104). While such an absurd argument is notable for its appearance in a serious journal of legal scholarship, maybe more serious is the characterization of the ubiquity of sexual abuse of as "demonstrably false" (ibid.). That portrayal is markedly different from the findings of the National Violence against Women Survey (see Tjaden and Thoennes 2000) and the National Intimate Partner and Sexual Violence Survey (see Black et al. 2011). And it is worlds apart from Hudson et al.'s (2012, 96–97) empirical estimation that globally the number of female deaths "due to societal devaluation of female life" in the twentieth century is greater than the total number of deaths from interstate war and civil conflict in that same century.

In 2012, Roger Schlafly, son of "pro–family values" warrior Phyllis Schlafly, lamented an initiative in the US Congress to reauthorize the 1994 federal Violence against Women Act (VAWA) by mocking a statement made by the bill's coauthor, Rep. Sandy Adams (R-FL). In her remarks on the House floor urging reauthorization, Representative Adams spoke about her own experience, saying, "The man I married had a penchant for drinking and was very violent when he drank." Mr. Schlafly's commentary is indicative of a common response to violence against women that we discuss throughout this book: blaming the victim. He asked dismissively, "Is VAWA going to somehow use federal law to protect women from marrying men who like to get drunk and crazy?" US Representative Gwen Moore (D-WI) stated on the floor that before VAWA became law, she felt that it was she, not her rapist, who was on trial in court; the way she dressed, her status as a single mother, and other factors unrelated to the rape were being used in court in an attempt to discredit her story (Tashman 2012). Schlafly posited,

So [Moore] testified in court that a man raped her, but did not want to answer questions about whether she seduced the man. She wants a federal law to presume that men are guilty so that female accusers do not have to answer embarrassing questions. (Schlafly 2012)

A corollary complaint is that the VAWA is simply an intentional loophole for immigrant women to get citizenship by making claims of abuse against their spouses. Despite this claim being as baseless as Schlafly's others—any woman who tried this route would need a police officer's testimony in support, and would be filing her claim within a system that is extremely wary of fraud (North 2012)—the Republican authors of the US House of Representatives' version of the VAWA reauthorization wrote into its original version a stipulation that the accused abuser had to be notified in the case of an immigrant woman's complaint of abuse. That clause was stricken from the final version of the bill, which nonetheless "rolls back current protections for immigrant women who are suffering from domestic abuse and workplace violence" (*Ms.* Magazine 2012). Not all the fire comes from males, though. Conservative scholar Janice Shaw Crouse wrote that VAWA "is all about restraining orders, arrests, prosecution, batterer intervention programs, fostering false allegations, re-educating judges in feminist ideology and biases, and law enforcement training that have been shown to increase, rather than decrease violence" (Crouse 2012).

In February 2013, the US House of Representatives reauthorized VAWA by a 286–134 vote. The bill had previously passed the Senate by a vote of 78–22. All of the votes against reauthorization were cast by Republicans. Lest we appear intentionally partisan, let it be clear that *any* party accounting for 100 percent of votes against anti–gender-violence legislation is an obstacle to the reduction of violence against women. Indeed, the extremity of views about VAW espoused by Republican candidates at some of the highest levels of elected office in the United States during the 2012 election year was shocking. A Republican Senatorial candidate from Missouri, Todd Akin., stated in a debate, "If [a rape is] a legitimate rape, the female body has ways to try to shut that whole thing down." Indiana state treasurer and Republican Senatorial candidate Richard Mourdock stated about six weeks later, also in a debate, that "even when life begins in that horrible situation of rape, that it is something that God intended to happen" (Madison 2012).

During the same election cycle, out of twenty-eight contested elections for the US Senate, twelve Republican nominations "went to candidates who would ban abortion even for survivors of sexual assault. That's a plurality of the party's primaries" (Saletan 2012). Apologism for violence against women is, unfortunately, not strictly an artifact of elections, however. The myth that women can simply walk away from abusive relationships or easily evade perpetrators of violence is both pervasive and corrosive. In early 2013, New Hampshire Republican state representative Mark Warden publicly supported a bill that would lessen penalties for domestic abusers, saying, "a lot of people like being in abusive relationships" and that "'people are always free to leave' abusive relationships" (Rayfield 2013).

Once again, the point of all this is that even in places that rate relatively highly for the strength of their VAW laws, much room for improvement remains. Further, and maybe more importantly, the fight to keep VAW-related laws strong and protective of women's recourse to justice in the face of sexual violence is an ongoing battle. A country's rating highly in our data does not indicate an absence of forces within that country seeking a reversal of existing protections.

We end this book with the unoriginal but learned caution that laws require enforcement and victims require readily available access to a constellation of services. But law needs more than that to go beyond being symptomatically responsive and begin addressing the structural underpinnings of violence against women. Our research made it clear that governments must ensure not only that women are aware of their rights, but also that men are aware of women's rights. Educating *all* citizens, irrespective of gender, about respecting the legally codified dignity of women as individuals—not just as components of social institutions such as religious bodies, communal groups, or marriages—is crucial. Only with such measures can law begin eroding traditional practices that operate outside of formal systems of justice that can be harmful or even deadly to women.

Appendix A

Additional Original Data

Aside from our four indicators addressing domestic legal guarantees, we created two original measures for the analyses in this book: enforcement of legal guarantees and the level of gender-violence-related societal discrimination. Here we briefly describe how these data were created.

Enforcement of Legal Guarantees

Law is most meaningful when applied in practice, and there exists great variation among countries in how well laws are enforced, so our indicator is ordinal in an attempt to categorize countries in this regard:

Enforcement of legal protections is
- (0) Rare/Nonexistent
- (1) Selective/Uneven
- (2) Routine/Effective

In creating our enforcement data, we did not find the same types or level of errors in the US State Department Country Reports on Human Rights Practices as we did for legal guarantees. Thus, we used this systematic annual report as our primary information source.

0: Rare/Nonexistent Enforcement

A country received the score of 0 (zero) for enforcement if its investigation and/ or prosecution of all four forms of violence against women (VAW) occurred rarely, not at all, or in a systematically ineffective manner.[1] Instances where the government or authorities "generally did not intervene," "did not enforce the law," "did not enforce provisions effectively," or "rarely took action" were coded as a 0, as were instances where VAW "frequently went unprosecuted" or perpetrators across all or most all forms of violence systematically received light sentences.

A country received a score of 0 where there was selective enforcement of a single form of violence against women but all other forms were generally not enforced. For our purposes, the Country Reports were deemed to indicate a lack of general enforcement in cases where the government or authorities are described as generally "unsympathetic" or "unwilling" to act in cases of violence against women.

1: Selective/Uneven Enforcement

A country received a score of 1 for enforcement if its investigation and/or prosecution of numerous forms of violence against women occurred sometimes, selectively, or not always effectively. General enforcement for any form of violence against women received a score of at least 1. If enforcement was described as "uneven" or "not always" effective, then selective enforcement was deemed to exist. Instances where authorities maintained a "wide degree of discretion in sentencing" also qualified as cases of selective enforcement.

A country received a score of 1 for enforcement in cases where a single form of violence against women was generally enforced or in cases where there was selective enforcement across numerous forms of violence against women. If authorities were failing or unwilling to investigate and/or prosecute occurrences of violence against women within one or more minority groups (rather than the general population), the country received a score of 1. We did not give countries a break for having weak institutions. Actual enforcement had to be demonstrable to affect the enforcement score for the year being coded—intent to enforce laws alone did not count toward a score.

2: Routine/Effective Enforcement

A country received a score of 2 if the Country Report indicated that it "generally" or "fully" enforced its laws pertaining to violence against women in a systematic fashion. It is important to note that a country could receive a 2 for enforcement even if some instances of violence against women still occur there, since VAW occurs in *all* countries. Instances where the government and/or authorities were described as having "generally" or "effectively" prosecuted violators of these laws, or were described as having "generally," "strictly," or "effectively" enforced laws against VAW received a 2. Additionally, a country received a score of 2 if there was selective enforcement of only a single form of violence against women but all other forms were generally enforced. Countries that consistently apply penalties for breaking laws prohibiting violence against women also received a score of 2.

Societal Discrimination

Countries where traditional and cultural practices result in high levels of discrimination severely disadvantage women in society. Thus, in any cross-country analysis it is important to know what societies are like in those countries in this regard. Using information from the State Department Country Reports on Human Rights Practices, we constructed the following indicator of levels of gender-violence-related societal discrimination against women. It is important to point out that this indicator measures only discrimination explicitly related to violence against women, not all forms of discrimination. We don't believe that other dimensions of discrimination are less important or unrelated to this one. Rather, this indicator reflects both a desire to measure the most germane forms of discrimination, as well as a nod to the limits of reliable measurement of societal discrimination.

VAW-related societal discrimination is the social acceptance of abuse against women in society. It can be formal or informal and refers to cultural, traditional, or customary practices that systematically discriminate against women. Culture, tradition, or custom may restrict women's freedom to report violence for fear of some form of reprisal or because persistent societal attitudes maintain that violence against women is a private rather than a public matter. VAW-related societal discrimination may also inhibit awareness or action that can be taken to protect women from violence, such as the arrest of women's-rights activists, or it may contribute to levels of violence against women that exist in a country in general.

> The level of VAW-related societal discrimination against women is
> (0) High
> (1) Moderate
> (2) Low to Nonexistent/Not Mentioned

0: High

Countries where traditional or cultural practices played a major role in violence against women received a 0 (zero), and underreporting of violence was a telltale sign of this situation. The Country Reports were clear about where there were few to no reports of violence against women for cultural reasons. In our coding scheme, a country received a score of 0 if, for any one or more forms of violence against women, most/all/many women were reluctant to report violence and/or testify against perpetrators of VAW *and* the Country Report explicitly states that this is because of social attitudes, including fear of reprisal/retribution, shame, honor, or other related reasons. For example, the Country Report may have indicated that cases of violence against women are "never reported," "typically," "commonly," "largely," "widely," or "often unreported" because of "stringent or severe societal reprisal," because "family members force female victims of violence to keep quiet," or as a "result of cultural or traditional stigma." These were indicative of high levels of VAW-related societal discrimination, and such countries received a score of 0.

Also, if a Country Report indicated that some form of violence was "widespread" because it was considered "socially acceptable," high levels of VAW-related societal discrimination exist and the country was coded as a 0. This includes the social acceptance of cultural practices that are violent toward women, such as dowry deaths, honor crimes, female genital mutilation, forced marriage, forced sterilization, and female infanticide.

Also, countries that exercised discriminatory punishment against women for reporting violence, including (but not limited to) fines, arrest, lashing, and imprisonment, indicated a high level of VAW-related societal discrimination and were coded as a 0.

Additionally, countries described as undergoing a "femicide" or "feminicide" received a score of zero, as these situations were assumed to be impossible to sustain without broad social support. Also, any country where women were described as being generally/widely viewed as property received a score of zero. Finally, countries where customary law superseded statute in a discriminatory manner against women in general (not just, for example, against one minority group) were coded as 0, as a high level of VAW-related societal discrimination exists to support that situation.

1: Moderate

In countries where traditional or cultural practices played a significant role in violence against women, a moderate level of VAW-related societal discrimination was deemed to exist, and these countries were coded as a 1. If the Country Report indicated, for any one or more forms of violence against women, that most/all/many women are reluctant to report violence and/or testify against perpetrators of VAW and the Country Report did not identify a reason for this underreporting, that country received a score of 1. Also, if a Country Report explicitly indicated that, for any one or more forms of violence against women, any/some women were reluctant to report/testify against perpetrators of VAW as a result of cultural/societal/traditional pressures, that country received a score of 1.

Particular attention was paid to key terms mentioned in the Country Reports. For example, when a report indicated that "in practice, familial and societal pressures occasionally discouraged women from seeking legal remedies," "women were at times reluctant to report rape for cultural reasons," or "women were sometimes humiliated by public officials for reporting violence" a moderate level of VAW-related societal discrimination was deemed to exist, and that country received a score of 1.

When societal discrimination in a country is limited to one or some female minority group(s) through the failure to report VAW as a result of cultural or traditional practices, a moderate level of VAW-related societal discrimination exists, and such countries were coded as a 1. Finally, any country where customary law supersedes statute in a discriminatory manner against women for one or some minority groups, and/or is enforced regionally or to a limited extent, was coded as a 1.

2: Low to Nonexistent/Not Mentioned

If a Country Report did not indicate that culture, tradition, or custom were problems or a means of increased violence against women, we assumed that societal discrimination was not significantly contributing to violence against women, and therefore little to no VAW-related societal discrimination exists. These countries were coded as a 2.

Appendix B

Multivariate Analysis

Model Choice

To statistically examine the hypotheses explaining the strength of legal protections against VAW, we use a stereotype logistic regression model. This model allows us to explain an ordinal (categorical) dependent variable. Our dependent variables represent a rank ordering of the strength of legal protections against gender-based violence, where a score of 3 is stronger than a score of 2, which is stronger than a score of 1, and so on. However, we can rank the scores of these variables only as stronger or weaker in comparison to one another, and we do not know exactly how much stronger a score of 3 is than a score of 2, or a score of 2 is than a score of 1. The stereotype logistical regression model we utilize in our analyses takes into account the rank ordering of the dependent variables examined here.[1] Given that the regression results (coefficients) from the ordered response model are not easily interpretable, we calculate substantive effects, including the predicted changes in the probability of adoption of strong legal guarantees as the explanatory variables change (increase).

To examine the hypotheses associated with the women's outcome dependent variables, we employ an ordinary least squares regression model. The women's-outcomes variables are measured at the ratio level (values are ranked *and* the distance between values is meaningful). Statistical models often assume that each observation—here, every country-year (i.e., Afghanistan 2001)—is independent of every other country-year (i.e., Afghanistan 2002). However, the strength of legal protections in any given country-year is likely not completely independent of the strength of legal protections in the preceding years. To account for non-independence within countries, we include standard errors clustered by country in each of the models.[2] This provides a more difficult test of the hypotheses by taking into account dependence across country-years. Our results are robust to alternative model specifications; more specifically, the incorporation of random effects in both models yields similar results to those specified previously.[3]

Dependent Variables

In a statistical analysis, the dependent variable is the variable whose quantity or quality one is seeking to explain. To test several different hypotheses, we use several dependent variables in our analyses. Our primary dependent variables are our original indicators of the strength of domestic legal protections against rape, marital rape, domestic violence, and sexual harassment. These are the same indicators whose construction we described in Chapter 4. For other analyses, we also use a dependent variable representing an index of overall legal protections against violence against women (presented in Table 5.3). This indicator is an additive index of our four original legal variables, so it ranges from 0 (no domestic legal protection from any of these four types of violence) to 12 (fullest domestic legal protection across all four types of violence). In our analyses we also examine a dependent variable capturing a country's enforcement of legal guarantees. This, too, is an original indicator created for this book, and its construction is described in detail in Appendix A. It ranges from 0 (no enforcement) to 2 (routine enforcement).

Finally, to assess the relationship between legal guarantees and women's outcomes/status, we use three well-known indicators as dependent variables. First, we use the United Nations Gender Inequality Index (GII), which is a composite index capturing the inequality in achievements between women and men along three dimensions, including reproductive health, empowerment, and the labor market. The GII ranges from 0 to 1, with lower values indicating greater equality between women and men, and higher values indicating greater inequality (United Nations Development Programme 2013). Second, we use the United Nations Human Development Index (HDI). The HDI is also a composite index, capturing three dimensions of human development: health, education, and living standards.[4] We expect that as the strength and enforcement of legal guarantees protecting women from violence increases, the level of human development also increases. The HDI is taken from the United Nations

Development Programme's World Development Reports and ranges from 0 to 1, with higher values indicating higher levels of development (United Nations Development Programme 2013). Finally, we employ as an indicator of women's health the percentage of women aged fifteen and over living with HIV/AIDS (out of all persons with HIV/AIDS in that country).[5]

Independent Variables

An independent variable is an indicator that seeks to explain the level of, or changes in, the dependent variable. To test our hypotheses we use several independent variables in our analyses. Table B.1 presents the independent variables we examine in the analysis: the concept the variable is intended to capture, the operationalization of the variable (the way the variable is coded), and the source of the data.

To account for the numerous possible alternative explanations of our dependent variables, we use a number of independent variables in our statistical analyses, including women's political participation, women's economic rights, women's economic empowerment,[6] economic globalization, social/cultural pressure, religious pressure, international law and social movements,[7] regional diffusion,[8] civil war, resistance to international law, democracy, and state capacity.

Table B.1

Independent Variable	Operationalized	Source
Women's political participation	Percentage of women in parliament	Inter-Parliamentary Union's Women in National Parliament Statistical Archive (2013)
Civil war	Presence of civil war (coded 1) or absence of civil war (coded 0)	Gleditsch et al. (2002)
Women's economic rights	Law and practice pertaining to women's economic rights (range of 0–3; higher values indicate greater economic rights)	CIRI women's economic rights indicator (Cingranelli and Richards (2010))
Women's economic empowerment	Total fertility rate	World Bank World Development Indicators (2013)
Economic globalization	Merchandise trade (sum of merchandise exports and imports divided by the value of GDP, all in current US dollars)	World Bank World Development Indicators (2013)
Cultural/social pressure	Societal discrimination (range of 0–2, with lower values indicating greater societal discrimination)	Richards and Haglund (2013)
Religious pressure	Majority-Muslim and majority-Christian country (coded 1 where the majority of the population identifies with one of these religious traditions and 0 otherwise for each religious tradition)	Richards and Haglund (2013)
International law/strength of women's movements	Number of years for which a country has been a party to the CEDAW treaty	United Nations Treaty Collection Database (2013)
Regional diffusion of laws	Mean VAW legal protection score for all contiguous countries	Weidmann, Kuse, and Gleditsch (2010)
VAW legal protections	Strength of VAW legal protections (range of 0–12 and includes strength of sexual harassment, rape, domestic violence, and marital rape laws)	Richards and Haglund (2013)

(continued)

Table B.1 *(continued)*

Independent Variable	Operationalized	Source
Resistance to international law	Reservation to Article 2 of the CEDAW treaty	Richards and Haglund (2013)
Substantive and procedural democracy	Strength of democratic-oriented empowerment rights (range of 0–14, with higher values indicating greater rights)	CIRI empowerment rights indicator (Cingranelli and Richards (2010))
Capacity	Gross national income (logged)	World Bank World Development Indicators (2013)
Trafficking legislation	Strength of trafficking legislation (range of 0–3, with higher values indicating stronger legislation)	Richards and Haglund (2013)

Notes

Introduction

1. Human rights are a means to attain and defend a life of human dignity. While the United Nations has never formally defined human dignity, in the UN's *Teaching Human Rights,* human rights are touted as providing the ability of humans to "develop fully and use our human qualities, our intelligence, our talents and our conscience and to satisfy our spiritual or other needs" (United Nations 2004, 9).

Chapter 1

1. See World Conference on Human Rights, Vienna Declaration and Programme of Action, UN Doc. A/CONF.157/23, 12 July 1993, Pt. 1, para. 18.

2. See UN Declaration on the Elimination of Violence against Women 1993 (DEVAW), GA res. A/RES/48/104, 20 December 1993.

3. See DEVAW and World Conference on Women, Beijing Declaration and Platform for Action, UN Doc. A/CONF.177/20 (1995) and A/CONF.177/20/Add.1 (1995), Pt. D.

4. CEDAW Committee, General Recommendation No. 19, 11th Session, 1992.

5. See *Opuz v. Turkey* (Judgment, Merits and Just Satisfaction, 2009).

6. The tension of state involvement in the private sphere represents a global phenomenon, not restricted solely to Turkey. For example, the Inter-American Commission on Human Rights ruled in July 2011, with respect to a 2005 Supreme Court case (*Town of Castle Rock, Colorado v. Gonzales),* that the United States needed to do more to protect victims of domestic violence (Wilson 2011). This case is addressed in more detail in Chapter 3.

7. Further, the most rigorous empirical research indicates that 2–8 percent of reported cases of rape are falsely reported (Kelly, Lovett, and Regan 2005; Lonsway, Archambault, and Lisak 2009).

8. See McCue (2008) for a more extensive examination of each type of violence.

Chapter 2

1. Both descriptive and substantive representation arguments have been made by scholars with reference to other minority groups in government, as well.

2. This argument can be made with respect to members of most social groups. Social identities may shift and change over time and across groups, making identification with one group more or less important, depending on the time and context relevant to individuals within the group (Fraser 1992).

3. See Chapter 1 for further discussion of gender-based violence (particularly rape) during and following armed conflict.

4. See Merry (2006) for further discussion of cultural practices related to violence against women.

5. Richards and Gelleny (2007) differentiate between the status of women in reference to a collection of rights and duties in international law and the status of women as relative to men, an approach the United Nations has taken in many of its development indicators. They define women's status as "the extent to which women are able, both in an absolute and relative sense, to exercise precise rights, codified in a large body of international human rights law and to enjoy the objectives of those rights" (856).

Chapter 3

1. This list of regional treaties is illustrative, not exhaustive. For a comprehensive overview, see the "Prevention of Violence against Women and Girls" reports provided annually by the United Nations Commission on the Status of Women: http://www .un.org/womenwatch/daw/csw/session.htm.

2. See the 1979 Convention on the Elimination of All Forms of Discrimination against Women, "Introduction." http://www.un.org/womenwatch/daw/cedaw/text /econvention.htm.

3. Emphasis in the original. http://www.un.org/womenwatch/daw/cedaw/text /econvention.htm.

4. *Case 12.626, Inter-American Commission on Human Rights, Report No. 80/11.*

5. (04–278) 545 U.S. 748 (2005).

6. Jessica Gonzales changed her name to Jessica Lenahan between the Supreme Court decision and the appeal to the Inter-American Commission.

7. [1992] LRC (Const) 628 (1992).

8. [1997] 3 LRC 361 (1997).

9. Emphasis in original.

10. Rhodesia is now called Zimbabwe.

11. Emphasis added.

12. While the term *objectivity* is widely studied and critiqued by feminists, the term *feminism* by no means represents a philosophically monolithic bloc of persons (Weldon 2006).

13. Emphasis added.

Chapter 4

1. Htun and Weldon's (2012) data on legal guarantees are also dichotomous, but differ from the UN data in that instead of representing the presence of "any" law, they note the presence of a "specialized" law. Our critique of the dichotomous UN measure applies to Htun and Weldon's data, as well, however.

2. A "correlative law situation" occurs when no laws are present that specifically prohibit a particular form of VAW but other laws exist that can be used to prosecute perpetrators of this form of violence.

3. This is not a purely hypothetical scoring scenario. One of the authors and a research assistant visited UN Women headquarters in New York in January 2013 and spoke at length with several staff members about this issue. They were told, unequivocally, that "any law" counts as a law for the purpose of the UN measure, no matter how bad that law may be. The UN Women staffers were aware of the consequences of this, but made clear that the UN member states they serve would never accept a more sophisticated measurement scheme. Unsurprisingly, it is in the political interest of member states to be shown having laws to protect women. Thus, the member states would not be happy about a measure that gets into the details of these laws and, consequently, makes some of them look poor in this regard, especially relative to their peers.

4. See the WomanStats Project Codebook at http://womanstats.org/Codebook Current.htm#psow.

5. Ibid.

6. Conceptualizations of each of these four forms of violence can be found in Chapter 1.

7. ICTR-96-4-T, Judgment 2 September 1998.

8. Bias is when an indicator is higher or lower than it should be because of the influence of something other than what the indicator is intended to measure.

9. For a list of these databases, see http://www.foreignlawguide.com/Frequently Cited Databases.htm.

10. See http://www.legislationline.org.

11. 2004 Cri LJ 2881.

12. CRL.REV.P. No. 321 of 2008.

Chapter 5

1. To define our regions and subregions, we use the designations provided by the United Nations Statistics Division, which can be found at *http://unstats.un.org/unsd /methods/m49/m49alpha.htm.*

2. We also investigated majority-Christian status. Were Figure 5.7 to show *majority-Christian states* rather than *non-majority-Muslim* states on the left side, the figure would look nearly identical to its present form. Eighty-four percent of our sample of countries are either majority Muslim or majority Christian, with the remaining few countries being majority Jewish, Buddhist, or animist, having a secular supermajority (e.g., Estonia), or other.

3. Formally, the empowerment index is a measure of government practices, not laws. However, our justification for using it as a proxy in this simple test is that these particular types of freedoms are, almost without exception, based on legal guarantees in a country's constitution, statutory law, or both. That is, here we assume that law exists if respect is practiced.

4. The assumption that needs to be met to establish sequence is known as double monotonicity.

Conclusion

1. In digesting this book's conclusions from its quantitative analyses, we ask readers to remember the socio-political world as it really is: probabilistic, not deterministic. That is, the world is largely one of chance, not certainty. Generalizations resulting from social-science analyses are routinely qualified by conditions such as "at these times" or "in these places." This does not render generalizations useless, however, as knowing things about parts of our world allows us to speak about our whole world in terms of likelihoods. Even phenomena widely regarded as axiomatic are often matters of likelihood, not destiny. For example, not all smokers end up contracting lung cancer, yet the general rule that smoking is extremely likely to result in lung cancer is of no small importance to both personal and public health. And so it is with socio-political phenomena such as laws.

Appendix A

1. Just because a country has no laws that specifically prohibit violence against women does not mean it automatically receives a score of 0 for enforcement, as some governments will prosecute violence against women under more-generalized laws against violence.

Appendix B

1. Conventional ordered logistic regression models make a restrictive assumption based on proportional odds. The proportional-odds restriction assumes that the effect of a

single set of covariates in constant across all categories of the dependent variable. The results of a likelihood ratio test and Brant test demonstrate that the proportional-odds assumption is indeed violated in our models. The stereotype logistic regression model removes this restriction. We ran ordered logistic regression models as robustness tests and the results are similar (in size and magnitude) to those from the stereotype logistic regression.

2. Nonindependence across countries is accounted for by including contiguity control variables in each model.

3. More specifically, we included random effects in the ordered logistic regression models that were examined in the robustness checks. We relied on the xtlogit command in Stata 13, and in the ordinary least squares regression models we relied on the xtreg command, specifying the "random effects" option. The direction and magnitude of the coefficients did not vary significantly from the original model specification.

4. The HDI relies on four indicators in order to capture the concepts of interest: life expectancy at birth, mean years of schooling, expected years of schooling, and gross national income per capita.

5. Data on HIV/AIDS are taken from UNAIDS (http://www.unaids.org/en/). Because data were estimates and available only for 2009, we followed Collier (2007) in using the 2009 score as a constant for the 2007–2010 window, as it represents a snapshot of a phenomenon that is not very dynamic year to year. Our female-life-expectancy data are from the World Bank's World Development Indicators dataset (2013).

6. We use fertility rate as a proxy for women's economic empowerment because various scholars suggest fertility rates often decline as women become increasingly likely to control reproductive decisions and as larger numbers of women enter the formal economic sphere (Furuoka 2009).

7. The number of years a country has been under the CEDAW treaty represents a proxy for not only the influence of international law, but also the strength of women's movements. Simmons (2009, 209) notes that "there is some plausibility to the argument that CEDAW ratification has had an influence on domestic policies by stimulating formation of women's organizations" and finds from her analyses evidence that indeed membership in women's organizations grows after CEDAW ratification. Htun and Weldon (2012, 554–555) offer a substantively rich, original measure of the autonomy and strength of women's movements, but, unfortunately, their data extend only to 2005 and so were not compatible with the timeframe of our study.

8. We created this variable using the CShapes package in R. Following Weidmann and Gleditsch (2010), we compute a distance matrix utilizing a 900km threshold to determine the relevant neighboring states. Countries meet the 900km distance threshold when the minimum distance between the two countries, or the distance between the two closest points from each country, is 900km or less. We then calculated the mean rape, marital rape, domestic violence, sexual harassment, total VAW legal protections, and enforcement of VAW legal protections for all contiguous states (those that meet the minimum distance threshold).

References

Abu-Odeh, Lama. 2011. "Crimes of Honor and the Construction of Gender in Arab Societies." *Comparative Law Review* 2(1): 1–47.

Acker, Joan. 2004. "Gender, Capitalism and Globalization." *Critical Sociology* 30(1): 24–46.

Agence France Press. 2014. "Indian Politician's 'Accidental Rape' Remark Adds to Rising Public Anger." *Guardian.* June 8. http://www.theguardian.com/world/2014/jun/08/indian-minister-rape-remark-anger-violence-women (Accessed July 2, 2014).

American Bar Association Central and East European Law Initiative. 2002. *The CEDAW Assessment Tool: An Assessment Tool Based on the Convention to Eliminate All Forms of Discrimination against Women.* http://apps.americanbar.org/rol/publications/assessment_tool_cedaw_tool_2002.pdf (Accessed December 7, 2012).

American Civil Liberties Union (ACLU). 2005. "ACLU Disappointed with Supreme Court Ruling on Domestic Violence Orders of Protection." June 27. http://www.aclu.org/womens-rights/aclu-disappointed-supreme-court-ruling-domestic-violence-orders-protection (Accessed October 15, 2012).

Amin, Sajeda, Ian Diamond, Ruchira T. Naved, and Margaret Newby. 1998. "Transition to Adulthood of Female Garment-Factory Workers in Bangladesh." *Studies in Family Planning* 29 (June): 185–200.

Amnesty International. 2001. *Broken Bodies, Shattered Minds: Torture and Ill-Treatment of Women.* London: Amnesty International. http://www.amnesty.org/en/library/asset/ACT40/001/2001/en/b68fe481-dc5f-11dd-bce7-11be3666d687/act400012001en.pdf (Accessed March 22, 2012).

———. 2004. "Rwanda: 'Marked for Death', Rape Survivors Living with HIV/AIDS in Rwanda." London: Amnesty International. http://www.amnesty.org/en/library/asset/AFR47/007/2004/en/53d74ceb-d5f7-11dd-bb24-1fb85fe8fa05/afr470072004en.pdf (Accessed January 28, 2013).

———. 2009. "Fact Sheet on Violence against Women in Armed Conflict." http://www
.amnestyusa.org/our-work/issues/women-s-rights (Accessed January 25, 2013).

Anderson, Siwan. 2003. "Why Dowry Payments Declined with Modernization in Europe
but Are Rising in India." *Journal of Political Economy* 111(2): 269–310.

An-Na'im, Abdullahi Ahmed. 1992. "Toward a Cross-Cultural Approach to Defining
International Standards of Human Rights: The Meaning of Cruel, Inhuman, or
Degrading Treatment or Punishment." In Abdullahi Ahmed An-Na'im, ed., *Human
Rights in Cross-Cultural Perspective: A Quest for Consensus*. Philadelphia: University
of Pennsylvania Press.

———. 2000. "Forced Marriage." Working paper, available at http://www.soas.ac.uk
/honourcrimes/resources/file55689.pdf (Accessed December 17, 2013).

Arnold, Kathryn Christine. 2001. "Are the Perpetrators of Honor Crimes Getting Away
with Murder? Article 340 of the Jordanian Penal Code Analyzed under the Convention on the Elimination of All Forms of Discrimination against Women." *American
University International Law Review* 16(5): 1343–1409.

Arzt, Donna E. 1990. "The Application of International Human Rights Law in Islamic
States." *Human Rights Quarterly* 12(2): 202–230.

Aust, Anthony. 2000. *Modern Treaty Law and Practice*. New York: Cambridge University Press.

Auster, Carol J., and Janel M. Leone. 2001. "Late Adolescents' Perspective on Marital
Rape: The Impact of Gender and Fraternity/Sorority Membership." *Adolescence*
36(141): 141–152.

Bachman, Jeff. 2012. "Protection from Sexual Violence Is a Human Right." *The
Hill: Congress Blog*. October 29, 2012. http://thehill.com/blogs/congress-blog
/presidential-campaign/264537-protection-from-sexual-violence-is-a-human-right
(Accessed October 29, 2012).

Baht, P. N. Mari, and Shiva S. Halli. 1999. "Demography of Brideprice and Dowry:
Causes and Consequences of the Indian Marriage Squeeze." *Population Studies*
53(2): 129–140.

Baker, Charlene K., Sarah L. Cook, and Fran H. Norris. 2003. "Domestic Violence and
Housing Problems: A Contextual Analysis of Women's Help-Seeking, Received Informal Support, and Formal System Response." *Violence against Women* 9(7): 754–783.

Banda, Fareda. 2005. *Women, Law and Human Rights*. Portland, OR: Hart Publishing.

Bartlett, Katharine T. 1990. "Feminist Legal Methods." *Harvard Law Review* 103(4):
829–888.

Basile, Kathleen C. and Michele C. Black. 2011. "Intimate Partner Violence against
Women." In Claire M. Renzetti, Jeffrey L. Edleson, Raquel K. Bergen, eds., *Sourcebook on Violence against Women*. Washington, DC: Sage.

Bayefsky, Anne. 2001. *The UN Human Rights Treaty System: Universality at the Cross-
roads*. Kluwer Law International: The Hague.

Bell, Sam R., Tavishi Bhasin, K. Chad Clay, and Amanda Murdie. 2013. "Taking the Fight to Them: Neighborhood Human Rights Organizations and Domestic Protest." *British Journal of Political Science* 44(4): 853–875.

Berger, Ronald J., Patricia Searles, and W. Lawrence Neuman. 1988. "The Dimensions of Rape Reform Legislation." *Law and Society Review* 22(2): 329–357.

Bergeron, Suzanne. 2001. "Political Economy Discourses of Globalization and Feminist Politics." *Signs* 26(4): 983–1006.

Berry, Frances Stokes, and William D. Berry. 1999. "Innovation and Diffusion Models in Policy Research." In P. A. Sabatier, ed., *Theories of the Policy Process*. Boulder, CO: Westview.

Berry, J. W. 2008. "Globalisation and Acculturation." *International Journal of Intercultural Relations* 32(4): 328–336.

Beteta, Hanny Cueva. 2006. "What Is Missing in Measures of Women's Empowerment?" *Journal of Human Development* 7(2): 221–241.

Bhagwati, Jagdish. 2004. *In Defense of Globalization*. Oxford: Oxford University Press.

Billig, Michael S. 1991. "The Marriage Squeeze on High-Caste Rajasthani Women." *Journal of South Asian Studies* 50(2): 341–360.

Black, Michele C., Kathleen C. Basile, Matthew J. Breiding, Sharon G. Smith, Mikel L. Walters, Melissa T. Merrick, Jieru Chen, and Mark R. Stevens. 2011. National Intimate Partner and Sexual Violence Survey (NISVS): 2010 Summary Report. Atlanta: National Center for Injury Prevention and Control, Centers for Disease Control and Prevention.

Blackstone, William. 1765. *Commentaries on the Law of England*. Oxford: Clarendon Press.

Blumel, Debra, G. L. Gibb, B. N. Innis, D. L. Justo and D. W. Wilson. 1993. "Who Pays? The Economic Costs of Violence against Women." Sunshine Coast: Sunshine Coast Interagency Research Group. Queensland: Women's Policy Unit, Office of the Cabinet.

Bob, Clifford. 2005. *The Marketing of Rebellion: Insurgents, Media, and International Activism*. New York: Cambridge University Press.

Bond, Johanna E. 2003. "International Intersectionality: A Theoretical and Pragmatic Exploration of Women's International Human Rights Violations." *Emory Law Journal* 52(1): 71–186.

Bonomi, Amy E., Robert S. Thompson, Melissa Anderson, Robert J. Reid, David Carrell, Jane A. Dimer, and Frederick Rivara. 2006. "Intimate Partner Violence and Women's Physical, Mental, and Social Functioning." *American Journal of Preventive Medicine* 30(6): 458–466.

Boushey, Graeme. 2010. *Policy Diffusion Dynamics in America*. Cambridge, UK: Cambridge University Press.

Braun, Yvonne A. 2010. "Gender, Development and Sex Work in Lesotho." *Equality, Diversity and Inclusion* 29(1): 78–96.

Breiding, Matthew J., Michele C. Black, George W. Ryan. 2008. "Prevalence and Risk Factors of Intimate Partner Violence in Eighteen U.S. States/Territories, 2005." *American Journal of Preventive Medicine* 34(2): 112–118.

Broderick, Elizabeth. 2012. "Working without Fear: Results of the Sexual Harassment National Telephone Survey." Sydney: Australian Human Rights Commission. https://www.humanrights.gov.au/working-without-fear-results-sexual-harassment-national-telephone-survey (Accessed June 20, 2014).

Brown, Wendy. 1995. *States of Injury: Power and Freedom in Late Modernity.* Princeton, NJ: Princeton University Press.

Brownmiller, Susan. 1975. *Against Our Will: Men, Women, and Rape.* New York: Simon and Schuster.

Brysk, Alison. "The Politics of Measurement: The Contested Count of the Disappeared in Argentina." *Human Rights Quarterly* 16(4): 676–692.

Bunch, Charlotte. 1990. "Women's Rights as Human Rights: Toward a Re-Vision of Human Rights." *Human Rights Quarterly* 12(4): 486–498.

———. 2012. "How Women's Rights Became Recognized as Human Rights." In Minky Worden, ed., *The Unfinished Revolution: Voices from the Global Fight for Women's Rights.* New York: Seven Stories Press, 29–40.

Caldwell, Barbara A., and Nancy Redeker. 2005. "Sleep and Tauma: An Overview." *Issues in Mental Health Nursing* 26(7): 721–738.

Campbell, J. C. 2002. "Health Consequences of Intimate Partner Violence." *Lancet* 359(9314): 1331–1336.

Campbell, Rebecca. 1998. "The Community Response to Rape: Victims' Experiences with the Legal, Medical, and Mental Health Systems." *American Journal of Community Psychology* 26(3): 355–379.

Campbell, Rebecca, and Sheela Raja. 1999. "Secondary Victimization of Rape Victims: Insights from Mental Health Professionals Who Treat Survivors of Violence." *Violence and Victims* 14(3): 261–275.

Campbell, Rebecca, and Stephanie Townsend. 2011. "Defining the Scope of Sexual Violence against Women." In Claire M. Renzetti, Jeffrey L. Edleson, and Raquel Kennedy Bergen, eds., *Sourcebook on Violence against Women.* Washington, DC: Sage.

Canadian Human Rights Commission. 1983. "Unwanted Sexual Attention and Sexual Harassment: Results of a Survey of Canadians." Ottawa: Research and Special Studies Branch, Canada.

Caprioli, Mary, and Kimberly Douglass. 2008. "Nation Building and Women: The Effect of Intervention on Women's Agency." *Foreign Policy Analysis* 4(1): 45–65.

Carbone-Lopez, Kristin, Candace Kruttschnitt, and Rose Macmillan. 2006. "Patterns of Intimate Partner Violence and Their Associations with Physical Health, Psychological Distress, and Substance Use." *Public Health Reports* 121(4): 382–392.

Carville, Olivia. 2012. "At The Dark End of the Street: The Lonely Death of Jill Meagher

Stirred Another Woman's Memories of a Chilling Night Encounter." September 30. *Sunday Age*. http://www.theage.com.au/victoria/at-the-dark-end-of-the-street -20120929-26skr.html (Accessed October 26, 2012).

Centers for Disease Control and Prevention (CDC). 2003. "Costs of Intimate Partner Violence against Women in the United States." Atlanta: Department of Health and Human Services, Centers for Disease Control and Prevention. http://www .cdc.gov/ncipc/pub-res/ipv_cost/ipvbook-final-feb18.pdf (Accessed February 1, 2013).

———. 2009. "Understanding Intimate Partner Violence: Fact Sheet." http://www .cdc.gov/ViolencePrevention/sexualviolence/definitions.html (Accessed January 14, 2013).

Chalk, Rosemary, and Patricia A. King. 1998. *Violence in Families: Assessing Prevention and Treatment Programs*. Washington, DC: National Academy Press.

Charlesworth, Hilary. 1999. "Feminist Methods in International Law." *American Journal of International Law* 93(2): 379–394.

Charlesworth, Hillary, and Christine Chinkin. 1993. "The Gender of Jus Cogens." *Human Rights Quarterly* 15(1): 63–76.

Chen, Martha, Joann Vanek, Francie Lund, James Heintz, Renana Jhabvala, and Christine Bonner. 2005. *Progress of the World's Women 2005: Women, Work, and Poverty*. United Nations Development Fund for Women. http://www.unwomen.org/en /digital-library/publications/2005/1/progress-of-the-world-s-women -2005-women-work-and-poverty (Accessed December 17, 2013).

Chesler, Phyllis. 2009. "Are Honor Killings Simply Domestic Violence?" *Middle East Quarterly* (Spring): 61–69.

Cingranelli, David L., and David L. Richards. 1999. "Measuring the Pattern, Level, and Sequence of Government Respect for Human Rights." *International Studies Quarterly* 43(3): 407–417.

———. 2010. "The Cingranelli and Richards (CIRI) Human Rights Data Project." *Human Rights Quarterly* 32(2): 401–424.

Cingranelli, David and Mikhail Filippov. 2010. "Electoral Rules and Incentives to Protect Human Rights." *Journal of Politics* 72(1): 1–15.

Cockburn, Cynthia. 2012. *Antimilitarism: Politics and Gender Dynamics of Movements to End War and Redefine Peace*. Basingstoke: Palgrave.

Coker, Ann L. 2007. "Does Physical Intimate Partner Violence Affect Sexual Health? A Systematic Review." *Trauma, Violence and Abuse* 8(2): 149–177.

Coker Ann L. and Donna L. Richter. 1998. "Violence against Women in Sierra Leone: Frequency and Correlates of Intimate Partner Violence and Forced Sexual Intercourse." *African Journal of Reproductive Health* 2(1): 61–72.

Coker, Ann L., Keith E. Davis, Ileana Arias, Sujata Desai, Maureen Sanderson, Heather M. Brandt, and Paige H. Smith. 2002. "Physical and Mental Health Effects of

Intimate Partner Violence for Men and Women." *American Journal of Preventive Medicine* 23(4): 260–268.

Cole, Alison. 2010. "International Criminal Law and Sexual Violence: An Overview." In Clare McGlynn and Vanessa E. Munro, eds., *Rethinking Rape Law: International and Comparative Perspectives.* New York: Routledge.

Conley, John M. 2011. "Comment." *Current Anthropology* 52(S3): S93–S94.

Conway, Margaret, David Ahern, and Gertrude Steurnagel. 1995. *Women and Public Policy: A Revolution in Progress.* Washington, DC: CQ Press.

Copelon, Rhonda. 1994. "Recognizing the Egregious in the Everyday: Domestic Violence as Torture." *Columbia Human Rights Law Review* 25(291): 291–367.

———. 2003. "International Human Rights Dimensions of Intimate Partner Violence: Another Strand in the Dialect of Feminist Law Making." *Journal of Gender, Social Policy and the Law* 11(2): 865–876.

Council of Europe Parliamentary Assembly Committee on Equal Opportunities for Women and Men. 2009. "Rape of Women, Including Marital Rape." http://assembly .coe.int/ASP/Doc/XrefViewHTML.asp?FileID=12324&Language=EN (Accessed August 5, 2013).

Crocker, Diane and Valery Kalembra. 1999. "The Incidence and Impact of Women's Experiences of Sexual Harassment in Canadian Workplaces." *Canadian Review of Sociology and Anthropology* 36(4): 541–558.

Crotty, James, Gerald Epstein, and Patricia Kelly. 1998. "Multinational Corporations in the Neo-Liberal Regime." In Dean Baker, Gerald Epstein, and Robert Pollin, eds., *Globalization and Progressive Economic Policy.* Cambridge, UK: Cambridge University Press.

Crouse, Janice Shaw. 2012. "A Bad Law on Life Support." *American Thinker.* March 5. http://www.americanthinker.com/2012/03/a_bad_law_on_life_support.html (Accessed August 13, 2013).

Cueva Beteta, Hanny. 2006. "What Is Missing in Measures of Women's Empowerment?" *Journal of Human Development* 7(2): 221–241.

Dahlberg, Linda, and Etienne G. Krug. 2002. "Violence—A Global Public Health Problem." In *World Report on Violence and Health,* ed., Linda L. Dahlberg. Geneva: World Health Organization.

Das Gupta, Monica. 1994. "Selective Discrimination against Female Children in Rural Punjab, India." *Population and Development Review* 13(1): 77–100.

Das Gupta, Monica, and P. N. Mari Bhat. 1998. "Intensified Gender Bias in India: A Consequence of Fertility Decline." In Maithreyi Krishnaraj and Ratna M. Sudashan, eds., *Gender, Population and Development.* Delhi: Oxford University Press.

Davenport, Christian. 1995. "Multidimensional Threat Perception and State Repression: An Inquiry into Why States Apply Negative Sanctions." *American Journal of Political Science* 39(3): 683–713.

———. 2007. *State Repression and the Domestic Democratic Peace.* New York: Cambridge University Press.

Davenport, Christian, and David Armstrong. 2004. "Democracy and the Violation of Human Rights: A Statistical Analysis from 1976–1996." *American Journal of Political Science* 48(3): 538–54.

Day, Tanis. 1995. "The Health Related Costs of Violence against Women in Canada: The Tip of the Iceberg." Centre for Research on Violence against Women and Children. London, Ontario. http://www.learningtoendabuse.ca/sites/default/files/pub_day1995.pdf (Accessed December 17, 2013).

Day, Tanis, Katherine McKenna, and Audra Bowlus. 2005. "The Economic Costs of Violence against Women: An Evaluation of the Literature." Expert Brief Compiled in Preparation for the Secretary-General's In-Depth Study on All Forms of Violence against Women. United Nations: Geneva, Switzerland. http://www.un.org/womenwatch/daw/vaw/expert%20brief%20costs.pdf (Accessed February 27, 2013).

Deo, Nandini. 2006. "Is Globalization Our Friend? Women's Allies in the Developing World." *Current History* 105(689): 105–111.

Deolalikar, Anil B., and Rao Vijayendra. 1998. "The Demand for Dowries and Bride Characteristics in Marriage: Empirical Estimates for Rural South Central India." In Maithreyi Krishnaraj and Ratna M. Sudashan, eds., *Gender, Population and Development.* Delhi: Oxford University Press.

Deveny, Catherine. 2012. "Jill Meagher. If Like Me You Thought Your Information Was Inconsequential Please Call Crimestoppers 1 800 333 000." September 27. http://www.catherinedeveny.com/columns/2012/9/27/jill-meagher-if-like-me-you-thought-your-information-was-inc.html (Accessed October 26, 2012).

Divekar, Sheila A., Gopu Natarajan, A. C. Ganguli and V. N. Purandare. 1979. "Abortion in Unmarried Girls." *Health and Population Perspectives and Issues* 2(4): 308–321.

Dodson, L. Debra, and Susan J. Carroll. 1991. *Reshaping the Agenda: Women in State Legislatures.* New Brunswick, N.J.: Center for American Women and Politics.

Drezner, Daniel. 2001. Globalization and Policy Convergence. *International Studies Review,* 3(1): 53–78.

Dudley, Margaret G., and Frederick A. Kosinski. 1990. "Religiosity and Marital Satisfaction: A Research Note." *Review of Religious Research* 32(1): 78–86.

Duflo, Esther. 2003. "Grandmothers and Granddaughters: Old Age Pension and Intra-Household Allocation in South Africa." *World Bank Economic Review* 17(1): 1–25.

Edwards, Alice. 2011. *Violence against Women under International Human Rights Law.* New York: Cambridge University Press.

Ehrlich, Sean D. 2007. "Access to Protection: Domestic Institutions and Trade Policy in Democracies." *International Organization* 61(3): 571–605.

Eichengreen, Barry. 1997. "The Tyranny of the Financial Markets." *Current History* 96 (November): 377–382.

Ellison, Christopher G., John P. Bartowski, and Kristin L. Anderson. 1999. "Are There Religious Variations in Domestic Violence?" *Journal of Family Issues* 20(1): 87–113.

Elman, Amy R. 1996a. *Sexual Politics and the European Union: The New Feminist Challenge*. Providence: Berghahn.

———. 1996b. *Sexual Subordination and State Intervention: Comparing Sweden and the United States*. Providence/Oxford: Berghahn.

Eriksson Baaz, Maria, and Maria Stern. 2009. "Why Do Soldiers Rape? Masculinity, Violence and Sexuality in the Armed Forces in the Congo (DRC)." *International Studies Quarterly* 53(2): 495–518.

Estrich, Susan. 1987. *Real Rape: How the Legal System Victimizes Women Who Say No*. Cambridge, MA: Harvard University Press.

Faley, Robert H., Deborah Erdos Knapp, Gary A. Kustis, and Cathy L. Z. Dubois. 1999. "Estimating the Organizational Costs of Sexual Harassment: The Case of the U.S. Army." *Journal of Business and Psychology* 13(4): 461–484.

Fang, Xiangming, and Phaedra Corso. 2008. "Gender Differences in the Connections between Violence Experienced as a Child and Perpetration of Intimate Partner Violence in Young Childhood." *Journal of Family Violence* 23(5): 303–313.

Feldner, Yotam. 2000. "'Honor' Murders—Why the Perps Get off Easy." *Middle East Quarterly* 8(4): 41–50.

Ferguson, John. 2012. "Domestic Violence Laws to be Hardened." *Australian: Victorian Country Edition*. October 7.

Ferris-Rotman, Amie, and Mirwais Harooni. 2012. "Afghan Teen Murder Spotlights Growing Violence against Women." *Reuters*. July 16. http://www.reuters.com/article/2012/07/16/us-afghanistan-women-killing-idUSBRE86F0CD20120716 (Accessed October 26, 2012).

Finkelhor, David, and Kersti Yllo. 1985. *License to Rape: Sexual Abuse of Wives*. New York: The Free Press.

Fontes, Lisa Aronson, and Kathy A. McCloskey. 2011. "Cultural Issues in Violence against Women." In Claire M. Renzetti, Jeffrey L. Edleson, and Raquel Kennedy Bergen, eds., *Sourcebook on Violence against Women*. Washington, DC: Sage.

Fischer, Karla. 1989. "Defining the Boundaries of Admissible Expert Testimony on Rape Trauma Syndrome." *University of Illinois Law Review* 3: 691–734.

Franklin, James C. 2008. "Shame on You: The Impact of Human Rights Criticism on Political Repression in Latin America." *International Studies Quarterly* 52(1):187–211.

Fraser, Nancy. 1992. "The Uses and Abuses of French Discourse Theories for Feminist Politics." In Nancy Fraswer and Sandra Lee Bartky, eds., *Revaluing French Feminism: Critical Essays on Difference, Agency, and Culture*. Bloomington: Indiana University Press.

Frese, Bettina, Miguel Moya, and Jesus L. Megias. 2004. "Social Perception of Rape:

How Rape Myth Acceptance Modulates the Influence of Situational Factors." *Journal of Interpersonal Violence* 19(2): 143–161.

Furuoka, Fumitaka. 2009. "Looking for a J-Shaped Development-Fertility Relationship: Do Advances in Development Really Reverse Fertility Declines?" *Economics Bulletin* 29(4): 3067–3074.

Garcia-Moreno, Claudia, and Christina Pallitto. 2013. "Global and Regional Estimates of Violence against Women: Prevalence and Health Effects of Intimate Partner and Non-Partner Sexual Violence." Geneva: Department of Reproductive and Health Research, World Health Organization.

Garrett, Geoffrey. 1998. "Partisan Politics in the Global Economy." Cambridge, UK: Cambridge University Press.

Gartland, Fiona. 2011. "Marital Rape Law Rejected Due to Family Concerns." *Irish Times* December 31, page 7.

Gavey, Nicola. 2005. *Just Sex? The Cultural Scaffolding of Rape.* London: Routledge.

Gelb, Joyce. 1989. *Feminism and Politics: A Comparative Perspective.* Berkeley: University of California Press.

Gentilviso, Chris. 2012. "Todd Akin On Abortion: 'Legitimate Rape' Victims Have 'Ways To Try To Shut That Whole Thing Down'." *Huffington Post.* August 19. http://www.huffingtonpost.com/2012/08/19/todd-akin-abortion-legitimate-rape_n_1807381.html (Accessed October 29, 2012).

Ghana Business News. 2012. "Women's Ministry Attacked for Non-Performance." December 19. http://www.ghanabusinessnews.com/2012/12/19/womens-ministry-attacked-for-non-performance/ (Accessed December 20, 2012).

Gielen, Andrea Carlson, Karen A. McDonnell, Jessica G. Burke, and Patricia O'Campo. 2000. "Women's Lives after an HIV-Positive Diagnosis: Disclosure and Violence." *Maternal and Child Health Journal* 4(2): 111–20.

Gies, Lieve. 2011. "The Hard Sell: Promoting Human Rights." *International Journal for the Semiotics of Law* 24(4): 405–422.

Gil-González, Diana, Carmen Vives-Cases, María Teresa Ruiz, Mercedes Carrasco-Portino, and Carlos Álvarex-Dardet. 2007. "Childhood Experiences of Violence in Perpetrators as a Risk Factor of Intimate Partner Violence: A Systematic Review." *Journal of Public Health* 30(1): 14–22.

Gleditsch, Nils Petter, Peter Wallensteen, Mikael Eriksson, Margareta Sollenbert, and Havard Strand. 2002. "Armed Conflict 1946–2001: A New Dataset." *Journal of Peace Research* 39(5): 615–637.

Goodman, Ryan, and Derek Jinks. 2004. "How to Influence States: Socialization and International Human Rights Law." *Duke Law Journal* 54(3): 621–703.

———. 2008. "Incomplete Internalization and Compliance with Human Rights Law." *European Journal of International Law* 19(4): 725–748.

Goodmark, Leigh. 2011. "State, National and International Legal Initiatives to Address

Violence against Women: A Survey." In Claire M. Renzetti, Jeffrey L. Edelson, and Raquel Kennedy, eds., *Sourcebook on Violence against Women*. Washington, DC: Sage, 191–208.

———. 2012. *A Troubled Marriage: Domestic Violence and the Legal System*. New York: New York University Press.

Gosper, Sophie. 2012. "Community Shaken by Random Nature of Killing of Jill Meagher." *Australian*. September 29. http://www.theaustralian.com.au/news /nation/community-shaken-by-random-nature-of-killing-of-jill-meagher/story -e6frg6nf-1226483787818 (Accessed October 29, 2012).

Gray, M. Mark, Miki Caul Kittilson, and Wayne Sandholtz. 2006. "Women and Globalization: A Study of 180 Nations, 1975–2000." *International Organization* 60(2): 293–333.

Greaves, Lorraine, Olena Hankivsky and Joanne Kingston-Reichers. 1995. "Selected Estimates of the Costs of Violence against Women." London, Ontario: Centre for Research on Violence against Women and Children Publication Series, University of Western Ontario. http://ywcacanada.ca/data/research_docs/00000025.pdf (Accessed February 27, 2013).

Greene, Malhotra, and Sanyukta Mathur. 2003. "Too Young To Wed." International Center for Research on Women, Washington, DC. http://www.icrw.org/files/publications /Too-Young-to-Wed-the-Lives-Rights-and-Health-of-Young-Married-Girls.pdf (Accessed December 17, 2013).

Greer, Edward. 2000. "Awaiting Cassandra: The Trojan Mare of Legal Dominance Feminism (Part I)." *Women's Rights Law Reporter* 21(2): 95–116.

Griffin, Susan. 1971. "Rape: The All-American Crime." *Ramparts* 10 (September): 26–35.

Gruber, James E. and Pheobe Morgan. 2005. *In the Company of Men: Male Dominance and Sexual Harassment*. Boston: Northeastern University.

Gupta, Ruchira. 2010. *Address to the Seminar on a Human Rights Approach to Combating Human Trafficking: Challenges and Opportunities; Implementing the Recommended Principles and Guidelines on Human Rights and Human Trafficking*. Geneva: United Nations Office of the High Commissioner for Human Rights, May 27–28, http:// www.facebook.com/note.php?note_id=10150197447835018 (Accessed December 17, 2013).

Gureyeva, Yuliya Aliyeva. 2012. "The Dynamics of Adoption of the Law on Domestic Violence in Azerbaijan: Gender Policy-Making in a Patriarchal Context." The Caucasus Research Resource Center Azerbaijan. http://www.academia.edu/5533568 /The_Dynamics_of_Adoption_of_the_Law_on_Domestic_Violence_in_Azerbaijan (Accessed January 10, 2013).

Hackett, Michelle. 2011. "Domestic Violence against Women: Statistical Analysis of Crimes across India." *Journal of Comparative Family Studies* 42(2): 267–288.

Hafner-Burton, Emilie M., and Kiyoteru Tsutsui. 2007. "Justice Lost! The Failure of International Human Rights Law to Matter Where Needed Most." *Journal of Peace Research* 44(4): 407–425.

Hamby, Sherry. L. and Mary P. Koss. 2003. "Shade of Gray: A Qualitative Study of Terms Used in the Measurement of Sexual Victimization." *Psychology of Women Quarterly* 27(3): 243–255.

Hansen, Gary L. 1987. "The Effect of Religiosity on Factors Predicting Marital Adjustment." *Social Psychology Quarterly* 50(3): 264–269.

Hardin, Jessica. 2013. "An Interview With Sally Engle Merry." *Anthropology News.* http://www.anthropology-news.org/index.php/2013/05/14/aes-in-todays-anthropology-3/ (Accessed July 2, 2014).

Hathaway, Oona A. 2002. "Do Human Rights Treaties Make a Difference?" *Yale Law Journal* 111(8): 1935–2042.

Hawkesworth, Mary. 2012. *Political Worlds of Women: Activism, Advocacy, and Governance in the Twenty-First Century.* Boulder, CO: Westview Press.

Hawkins, Darren, and Wade Jacoby. 2010. "Partial Compliance: A Comparison of the European and Inter-American Courts of Human Rights." *Journal of International Law and International Relations* 6: 35–85.

Heise, Lori L. 1998. "Violence against Women: An Integrated, Ecological Framework." *Violence against Women* 4(3): 262–290.

Heise, Lori L., Mary Ellsberg, Megan Gotemoeller. 1999. "Ending Violence against Women." *Population Reports.* Baltimore: Johns Hopkins University. http://www.vawnet.org/domestic-violence/summary.php?doc_id=272&find_type=web_desc_GC (Accessed December 17, 2013).

Heise, Lori and C. Garcia-Moreno. 2002. "Violence by Intimate Partners." In Etienne G. Krug, Linda Dahlberg, James A. Mercy, Anthony B. Zwi, and Rafael Lozano, eds., *World Report on Violence and Health.* Geneva: World Health Organization.

Helfer, Laurence R., and Erik Voeten. 2014. "International Courts as Agents of Legal Change: Evidence from LGBT Rights in Europe." *International Organization* 68(1): 77–110.

Hemmati, Minu, and Rosalie Gardiner. 2002. *Gender and Sustainable Development. World Summit Papers of the Heinrich Boll Foundation.* Germany: Heinrich Boll Foundation.

Her Majesty's Inspectorate of Constabulary (HMIC). 2007. "Without Consent: A Report on the Joint Review of the Investigation and Prosecution of Rape Offenses." London: Central Office of Information. http://www.hmic.gov.uk/media/without-consent-20061231.pdf (Accessed December 17, 2013).

Hertel, Bradley R., and Michael Hughes. 1987. "Religious Affiliation, Attendance, and Support for 'Pro-Family' Issues." *Social Forces* 65(3): 858–882.

Hertel, Shareen. 2006a. "New Moves in Transnational Advocacy: Getting Labor and

Economic Rights on the Agenda in Unexpected Ways." *Global Governance* 12(3): 263–281.

———. 2006b. *Unexpected Power: Conflict and Change among Transnational Activists.* Ithaca, NY: Cornell University Press.

Hesketh, Kanthryn, Susan Duncan, Carole Estabrooks, Marlene Reimer, Phyllis Giovanetti, Kathryn Hyndman, and Sonia Acorn. 2003. "Workplace Violence in Alberta and British Colombia Hospitals." *Health Policy* 63(3): 311–321.

Hevener, Natalie Kaufman. 1986. "An Analysis of Gender Based Treaty Law: Contemporary Developments in Historical Perspective." *Human Rights Quarterly* 8(1): 70–88.

Heyns, Christof H., and Frans Viljoen. 2001. "The Impact of the United Nations Human Rights Treaties on the Domestic Level." *Human Rights Quarterly* 23(3): 483–535.

Hillebrecht, Courtney. 2012. "The Domestic Mechanisms of Compliance with International Human Rights Law: Case Studies from the Inter-American Human Rights System." *Human Rights Quarterly* 34(4): 959–985.

Houston Chronicle News Services. 1992. "Acquittal of Husband Spurs Anger—Wife Accused Him of Raping Her." April 18. *Houston Chronicle,* 3A.

Htun, Mala, and S. Laurel Weldon. 2012. "The Civic Origins of Progressive Policy Change: Combating Violence against Women in Global Perspective, 1975–2005." *American Political Science Review* 106(3): 548–569.

Hudson, Valerie M., Bonnie Ballif-Spanvill, Mary Caprioli, and Chad F. Emmett. 2012. *Sex and World Peace.* New York: Columbia University Press.

Huen, Yuki. 2007. "Workplace Sexual Harassment in Japan." *Asian Survey* 47(5): 811–827.

Human Rights Watch. 2001. "Item 12—Integration of the Human Rights of Women and the Gender Perspective: Violence against Women and 'Honor' Crimes." Prepared for Human Rights Watch Oral Intervention at the 57th Session of the UN Commission on Human Rights. http://www.hrw.org/news/2001/04/05/item-12-integration -human-rights-women-and-gender-perspective-violence-against-women (Accessed March 22, 2012).

———. 2010. *Dignity on Trial: India's Need for Sound Standards for Conducting and Interpreting Forensic Examinations of Rape Survivors.* http://www.hrw.org/sites /default/files/reports/india0910webwcover.pdf (Accessed August 5, 2013).

Iaria, Melissa. 2010. "March Deplores Violence against Women." *The Australian.* October 20. http://www.theaustralian.com.au/news/latest-news/march-deplores-violence -against-women/story-fn3dxiwe-1226499949962 (Accessed October 13, 2014).

International Labor Organization (ILO). 1996. Declaration on Fundamental Principles and Rights at Work: Sexual Harassment at Work. Geneva: ILO. http://www.ilo.org /wcmsp5/groups/public/—-ed_norm/—-declaration/documents/publication /wcms_decl_fs_96_en.pdf (Accessed January 24, 2013).

———. 2012. "ILO 2012 Global Estimate of Forced Labour: Executive Summary." Geneva:

ILO. http://www.ilo.org/wcmsp5/groups/public/—-ed_norm/—-declaration /documents/publication/wcms_181953.pdf (Accessed December 17, 2013).

Inter-Parliamentary Union's Women in National Parliament Statistical Archive. 2013. Women in National Parliaments. http://www.ipu.org/wmn-e/classif-arc.htm (Accessed January 3, 2013).

Jahangir, Asma. 2000. "United Nations Report of the Special Rapporteur on Civil and Political Rights, Including Questions of Disappearances and Summary Executions. New York: United Nations.

Jewkes, Rachel. 2002. "Intimate Partner Violence: Causes and Prevention." *Lancet* 359 (April): 1423–1429.

Johnson, Holly, Natalia Ollus, and Sami Nevala. 2008. *Violence against Women: An International Perspective*. New York: Springer.

Jordan, Carol E. 2009. "Advancing the Study of Violence against Women: Evolving Research Agendas Into Science." *Violence against Women* 15 (January): 393–419.

Jovanavski, Valentina. 2012. "Avon Leads Charge on Criminalising Domestic Violence in Hungary." *Guardian*. December 12. http://www.guardian.co.uk/sustainable-business /avon-criminalising-domestic-violence-hungary (Accessed December 19, 2012).

Kabeer, Naila, and Simeen Mahmud. 2004. "Globalization, Gender, and Poverty: Bangladeshi Women Workers in Export and Local Markets." *Journal of International Development* 16 (January): 93–109.

Kalmuss, Debra, and Murray Straus. 1982. "Wife's Marital Dependence and Wife Abuse." *Journal of Marriage and the Family* 44(2): 277–286.

Kane-Urrabazo, Christine. 2007. "Sexual Harassment in the Workplace: It Is Your Problem." *Journal of Nursing Management* 15(6): 608–613.

Kang, Alice. 2011. "Bringing International Women's Rights Home." Paper presented at the Annual Meeting of the *American Political Science Association*. Seattle, WA. September 2.

Kapoor, Sushma. 2000. "Domestic Violence against Women and Girls." *Innocenti Digest* 6. UNICEFIRC. http://www.unicefirc.org/publications/pdf/digest6e.pdf (Accessed August 2, 2009).

Kapur, Ratna. 2005. *Erotic Justice: Law and the New Politics of Postcolonialism*. London: The Glass House Press.

Karega, Regina G. M. 2002. *Violence against Women in the Workplace in Kenya: Assessment of Workplace Sexual Harassment in the Commercial Agriculture and Textile Manufacturing Sectors in Kenya*. Washington, DC: International Labor Rights Fund. http://www.laborrights.org/sites/default/files/publications-and-resources/Kenya .pdf (Accessed December 17, 2013).

Kathlene, Lyn. 1994. "Power and Influence in State Legislative Policymaking: The Interaction of Gender and Position in Committee Hearing Debates." *American Political Science Review* 88(3): 560–576.

Keck, Margaret E., and Katherine Sikkink. 1998. *Activists beyond Borders: Advocacy Networks in International Politics.* Ithaca, NY: Cornell University Press.

Keith, Linda Camp. 1999. "The United Nations International Covenant on Civil and Political Rights: Does It Make a Difference in Human Rights Behavior?" *Journal of Peace Research* 36(1): 95–118.

Kelly, Liz, Jo Lovett, and Linda Regan. 2005. "A Gap or a Chasm? Attrition in Reported Rape Cases." Home Office Research Study 293. London, England: Home Office Research, Development and Statistics Directorate. http://webarchive.nationalarchives .gov.uk/20110218135832/rds.homeoffice.gov.uk/rds/pdfs05/hors293.pdf (Accessed December 17, 2013).

Kendall-Tackett, Kathleen A. 2007. "Inflammation, Cardiovascular Disease, and Metabolic Syndrome as Sequelae of Violence against Women: The Role of Depression, Hostility, and Sleep Disturbance." *Trauma, Violence, and Abuse* 8(2): 117–126.

Kersten, Joachim. 1996. "Culture, Masculinities and Violence against Women." *British Journal of Criminology* 36(3): 381–95.

King, Gary, Robert O. Keohane, and Sidney Verba. 1994. *Designing Social Inquiry: Scientific Inference in Qualitative Research.* Princeton, NJ: Princeton University Press.

Koh, Harold Hongju. 2005. "Internalization through Socialization." *Duke Law Journal* 54: 975–982.

———. 2007. "Is There a 'New' New Haven School of International Law?" *Yale Journal of International Law* 32: 559–573.

Koss, Mary P., Christine A. Gidycz, and Nadine Wisniewski. 1987. "The Scope of Rape: Incidence and Prevalence of Sexual Aggression and Victimization in a National Sample of Higher Education Students." *Journal of Consulting and Clinical Psychology* 55(2): 162–170.

Kurbanova, Manija. 2010. "Domestic Violence Bill Stalled in Tajikistan." *Institute for War and Peace Reporting* 632 (October 17). http://iwpr.net/report-news/domestic -violence-bill-stalled-tajikistan (Accessed August 5, 2013).

Lacey, Nicola. 2004. "Feminist Legal Theory and the Rights of Women." In Karen Knop, ed., *Gender and Human Rights.* Oxford: Oxford University Press.

Lakshmi, Rama. 2014. "Latest Alleged Gang Rape of Young Woman in India Highlights Vigilante Role of Village Elders." *Washington Post.* January 24. http://www .washingtonpost.com/world/asia_pacific/latest-gang-rape-of-young-woman-in -india-highlights-vigilante-role-of-tribal-village-elders/2014/01/24/80abe648 -84ef-11e3-a273-6ffd9cf9f4ba_story.html (Accessed January 24, 2014).

Landman, Todd. 2005. *Protecting Human Rights: A Comparative Study.* Washington, DC: Georgetown University Press.

Lang, Kylie. 2012. "We Can Help Stop Violence against Women by Changing Attitudes, Says Kylie Lang." *Herald Sun.* October 7. http://www.heraldsun.com.au/news

/national/we-can-help-stop-violence-against-women-by-changing-attitudes-says
-kylie-lang/story-fndo45rl-1226489720401 (Accessed October 26, 2012).

Lempert, Lora Bex. 1996. "Women's Strategies for Survival: Developing Agency in Abusive Relationships." *Journal of Family Violence* 11(3): 269–290.

Levinson, David. 1989. *Family Violence in Cross-Cultural Perspective.* Newbury Park, CA: Sage.

Lonsway, Kimberly A., and Joanne Archambault. 2012. "The 'Justice Gap' for Sexual Assualt Cases: Future Directions for Research and Reform." *Violence against Women* 18(2): 145–168.

Lonsway, Kimberly A., Joanne Archambault, and David Lisak. 2009. "False Reports: Moving beyond the Issue to Successfully Investigate and Prosecute Non-Stranger Sexual Assault." Alexandria, VA: The National Center for the Prosecution of Violence against Women. http://www.ndaa.org/pdf/the_voice_vol_3_no_1_2009.pdf (Accessed December 17, 2013).

Lovenduski, Joni, and Pippa Norris. 2003. "Westminster Women: The Politics of Presence." *Political Studies* 51(1): 84–102.

MacKinnon, Catherine A. 1979. *Sexual Harassment of Working Women.* New Haven: Yale University Press.

———. 2000. "Symposium on Unfinished Feminist Business: Some Points against Postmodernism." *Chicago-Kent Law Review* 75(3): 687–712.

———. 2006. *Are Women Human? And Other International Dialogues.* Cambridge, MA: Harvard University Press.

Macy, Rebecca. J., Joelle Ferron, and Carmen Crosby. 2009. "Partner Violence and Survivors' Chronic Health Problems: Informing Social Work Practice." *Social Work* 54(1): 29–43.

Macy, Rebecca J. Dania M. Ermentrout, and Natalie B. Johns. 2011. "Health Care for Survivors of Partner and Sexual Violence." In Claire M. Renzetti, Jeffrey L. Edleson, and Raquel Kennedy Bergen, eds., *Sourcebook on Violence against Women.* Washington, DC: Sage.

Madison, Lucy. 2012. "Richard Mourdock: Even Pregnancy from Rape Something 'God Intended'." *CBS News.* October 23. http://www.cbsnews.com/8301-250_162 -57538757/richard-mourdock-even-pregnancy-from-rape-something-god-intended/ (Accessed October 29, 2012).

Mahmood, Saba. 2005. *Politics of Piety: The Islamic Revival and the Feminist Subject.* Princeton: Princeton University Press.

Mahoney, James and Gary Goertz. 2006. "A Tale of Two Cultures: Contrasting Quantitative and Qualitative Research." *Political Analysis* 14(3): 227–249.

Maman, Suzanne, Jacquelyn Campbell, Michael Sweat, and Andrea C. Gielen. 2000. "The Intersection of HIV and Violence: Directions for Future Research and Interventions." *Social Science and Medicine* 50(4): 459–78.

Mardorossian, Carine M. 2002. "Toward a New Feminist Theory of Rape." *Signs* 27(3): 743–775.

Mayer, Ann Elizabeth. 2013. *Islam and Human Rights,* 5th ed. Boulder, CO: Westview Press.

McAllister, Ian, and Donley T. Studlar. 1992. "Region and Voting in Britain, 1979–87: Territorial Polarization or Artifact?" *American Journal of Political Science* 36(1): 168–199.

McCann, Deirdre. 2005. *Sexual Harassment at Work: National and International Responses.* Conditions of Work and Employment Programme, International Labor Organization, Geneva.

McCue, Margi Laird. 2008 *Domestic Violence: Second Edition.* ABC–CLIO: Denver, CO.

McDaniel, Morgan. 2013. "From Morocco to Denmark: Rape Survivors around the World Are Forced to Marry Attackers." May 2. http://www.womenundersiegeproject.org /blog/entry/from-morocco-to-denmark-rape-survivors-around-the-world-are -forced-to-marry (Accessed August 5, 2013).

McLean, Robyn, and Jane Goodman-Delahunty. 2008. "The Influence of Relationship and Physical Evidence on Police Decision-Making in Sexual Assault Cases." *Australian Journal of Forensic Sciences* 40(2): 109–121.

McMahon, Sarah. 2011. "Changing Perceptions of Sexual Violence Over Time." Harrisburg, PA: VAWnet, a project of the National Resource Center on Domestic Violence. http://www.vawnet.org (Accessed January 14, 2013).

Medicins Sans Frontieres/Doctors without Borders. 2009. *Shattered Lives: Immediate Medical Care Vital for Sexual Violence Victims.* Brussels: Doctors without Borders. http://www.doctorswithoutborders.org/publications/article.cfm?id=3422 (Accessed January 25, 2013).

Meloy, Michelle L., and Susan L. Miller. 2011. *The Victimization of Women: Law, Policies, and Politics.* New York: Oxford University Press.

Merry, Sally Engle. 2003. "Constructing a Global Law—Violence against Women and the Human Rights System." *Law and Social Inquiry* 28(4): 941–977.

———. 2006. *Human Rights and Gender Violence: Translating International Law into Local Justice.* Chicago: University of Chicago Press

———. 2011. "Measuring the World: Indicators, Human Rights, and Global Governance." *Current Anthropology* 52(S3): S83–S95.

Merry, Sally Engle, and Jessica Shimmin. 2011. "The Curious Resistance to Seeing Domestic Violence as a Human Rights Violation in the United States." In Shareen Hertel and Kathryn Libal, eds., *Human Rights in the United States: Beyond Exceptionalism.* Cambridge, UK: Cambridge University Press, 113–131.

Miguez, Liliana Silva. 2009. "The Efficiency of Legislation Enacted to Face Harmful Acts against Women in Latin America and the Caribbean." Paper Prepared for Expert Group Meeting on Good Practices in Legislation to Address Harmful Practices against

Women. United Nations Division for the Advancement of Women, United Nations Economic Commission for Africa. EGM/GPLHP/2009/EP.13.

Miller, Ted. R., Mark A. Cohen and Brian Wiersma. 1996. *Victim Costs and Consequences: A New Look*. Washington: National Institute of Justice.

Milner, Helen V., and Keiko Kubota. 2005. "Why the Move to Free Trade? Democracy and Trade Policy in the Developing Countries." *International Organization* 59(1): 107–143.

Mokken, R. J. 1971. *A Theory and Procedure of Scale Analysis*. Netherlands: Mouton and Co.

Morgan, Phoebe, and James E. Gruber. 2008. "Sexual Harassment and Male Dominance: Toward an Ecological Approach." In Michele A. Paludi, ed., *The Psychology of Women at Work: Obstacles and the Identify Jungle*. Westport, CT: Praeger.

———. 2011. "Sexual Harassment: Violence against Women at Work and in Schools." In Claire M. Renzetti, Jeffrey L. Edleson, and Raquel Kennedy Bergen, eds., *Sourcebook on Violence against Women*. Washington, DC: Sage.

Morken, Kristin, and Per Selle. 1995. "An Alternative Movement in 'State-Friendly' Society: The Women's Shelter Movement." In Lauri Karvonen and Per Selle, eds., *Women in Nordic Politics: Closing the Gap*. Aldershot, England: Dartmouth.

Morrison, Andrew R., and María Beatriz Orlando. 1999. "Social and Economic Costs of Domestic Violence: Chile and Nicaragua." In Andrew Morrison and María Beatriz Orlando, eds., *Too Close to Home: Domestic Violence in the Americas*. New York: Inter-American Development Bank.

Mosely, Layna and Saika Uno. 2007. "Racing to the Bottom or Climbing to the Top? Economic Globalization and Collective Labor Rights." *Comparative Political Studies* 40(8): 923–948.

Ms. Magazine. 2012. "House Passes Cantor/Adams VAWA Reauthorization." *Feminist Wire Newsbriefs*. May 17. http://www.msmagazine.com/news/uswirestory.asp?ID=13654 (Accessed October 29, 2012).

Munro, Vanessa E. 2010. "From Consent to Coercion: Evaluating International and Domestic Frameworks for the Criminalization of Rape." In Clare McGlynn and Vanessa E. Munro, eds., *Rethinking Rape Law: International and Comparative Perspectives*. New York: Routledge.

Murray, William, Nagaraj Sivasubramaniam, and Paul Jacques. 2001. "Supervisory Support, Social Exchange Relationships and Sexual Harassment Consequences." *Leadership Quarterly* 12(1): 1–29.

Narayan, Uma. 1997. *Dislocating Cultures: Identities, Traditions, and Third World Feminism*. New York: Routledge.

Nason-Clark, N. 1997. *The Battered Wife: How Christians Confront Family Violence*. Louisville, KY: Westminster/John Knox.

National Center for Injury Prevention and Control. 2003. "Costs of Intimate Partner Violence against Women in the United States." Atlanta: Centers for Disease Control and Prevention. http://www.cdc.gov/ncipc/pub-res/ipv_cost/ipvbook-final-feb18 .pdf (Accessed February 27, 2013).

Neumayer, Eric. 2005. "Do International Human Rights Treaties Improve Respect for Human Rights?" *Journal of Conflict Resolution* 49(6): 925–953.

———. 2007. "Qualified Ratification: Explaining Reservations to International Human Rights Treaties." *Journal of Legal Studies* 36(2): 397–429.

Niarchos, Catherine N. 2006. "Women, War, and Rape: Challenges Facing the International Tribunal for the Former Yugoslavia." In Bert B. Lockwood, ed., *Women's Rights: A Human Rights Quarterly Reader*. Baltimore: Johns Hopkins University Press.

Nigeria. 2013. *Criminal Code Act, Chapter 77, Laws of the Federation of Nigeria 1990*. http://www.nigeria-law.org/Criminal%20Code%20Act-PartI-II.htm (Accessed August 5, 2013).

Norris, Pippa. 1996. "Mobilizing the Women's Vote: The Gender-Generation Gap in Voting Behavior." *Parliamentary Affairs* 49(2): 333–342.

North, Anna. 2012. "Violence against Women Act Gives 'Men's Rights' Its Moment." *BuzzFeed*. May 17. http://www.buzzfeed.com/annanorth/violence-against-women -act-gives-mens-rights-it (Accessed October 29, 2012).

Nowrojee, Binaifer. 1996. "Shattered Lives: Sexual Violence during the Rwandan Genocide and Its Aftermath." Human Rights Watch Africa. http://www.hrw.org /reports/1996/Rwanda.htm (Accessed January 25, 2013)

OECD Development Centre. 2012a. 2012 SIGI Social Institutions and Gender Index. http://genderindex.org (Accessed August 17, 2014).

———. 2012b. "2012 SIGI Social Institutions and Gender Index: Data." http:// genderindex.org/content/data (Accessed August 5, 2013).

Office of the United Nations High Commissioner for Human Rights. 2012. "Convention on the Elimination of All Forms of Discrimination against Women New York, 18 December 1979." http://www.ohchr.org/en/ProfessionalInterest/pages/cedaw .aspx (Accessed August 18, 2012).

Okin, Susan Moller. 1981. "Liberty and Welfare: Some Issues in Human Rights Theory." In Roland J. Pennock and John W. Chapman, eds., *Human Rights*. New York: New York University Press.

O'Leary, K. Daniel. 1999. "Psychological Abuse: A Variable Deserving Critical Attention in Domestic Violence." *Violence and Victims* 14(1): 3–23.

Organization of American States Inter-American Commission on Human Rights. 1948. American Declaration of the Rights and Duties of Man. Adopted by the Ninth International Conference of American States, Bogotá, Colombia. http://www.cidh .oas.org/Basicos/English/Basic2.american%20Declaration.htm (Accessed August 16, 2014).

———. 2007. "Access to Justice for Women Victims of Violence in the Americas." OEA/Ser.L/V/II. Doc. 68. Washington, DC: General Secretariat, Organization of American States. http://www.cidh.org/women/Access07/Report%20Access%20 to%20Justice%20Report%20English%20020507.pdf (Accessed October 15, 2012).

———. 2011. "Merits: Jessica Lenahan (Gonzales) et al. v United States." July 21. Report No. 80/11 Case 12 626. www.oas.org/en/iachr/decisions/2011/USPU12626EN .doc (Accessed October 15, 2012).

Paul, Madan C. 1985. *Dowry and Position of Women in India: A Study of Delhi Metropolis.* New Delhi: Inter-India Pubs.

Pavey, Ainsley. 2012. "Family Violence Laws Changed to Protect Kids Like Darcey." *Courier Mail* June 2.

Pearson, Ruth. 2003. "Feminist Responses to Economic Globalization: Some Examples of Past and Future Practice." *Gender and Development* 11(1): 25–34.

Peek, Charles W., George D. Lowe, and L. Susan Williams. 1991. "Gender and God's Word: Another Look at Religious Fundamentalism and Sexism." *Social Forces* 69(4): 1025–1221.

Persson, Torsten, and Guido Enrico Tabellini. 2003. *The Economic Effects of Constitutions.* Cambridge, MA: MIT Press.

Peterson, V. Spike. 2003. *A Critical Rewriting of Global Political Economy.* New York: Routledge.

Phillips, Anne. 1998. *Feminism and Politics.* Oxford: Oxford University Press.

Pitkin, Hanna Fenichel. 1967. *The Concept of Representation.* Berkeley: University of California Press.

Poe, Steven, and C. Neal Tate. 1994. "Repression of Personal Integrity Rights in the 1980s: A Global Analysis." *American Political Science Review* 88(4): 853–72.

Postmus, Judy. L, Margaret Severson, Marianne Berry, and Jeong Ah Yoo. 2009. "Women's Experiences of Violence and Seeking Help." *Violence against Women* 15(7): 852–868.

Powell, G. Bingham. 2000. *Elections as Instruments of Democracy: Majoritarian and Proportional Visions.* New Haven, CT: Yale University Press.

Prewitt, Shauna R. 2010. "Giving Birth to a 'Rapist's Child': A Discussion and Analysis of the Limited Legal Protections Afforded to Women Who Become Mothers through Rape." *Georgetown Law Journal* 98(3): 827–862.

Rao, Aruna, and David Kelleher. 2005. "Is There Life After Gender Mainstreaming?" *Gender and Development* 13(2): 57–69.

Rayfield, Jillian. 2013. "People Like Being in Abusive Relationships." *Salon.* February 27. http://www.salon.com/2013/02/27/n_h_goper_a_lot_of_people_like_being _in_abusive_relationships/ (Accessed August 13, 2013).

Reeves, Audrey. 2011. "Senegal." Geneva Centre for the Democratic Control of

Armed Forces. http://www.dcaf.ch/content/download/47666/710362/file/14
_Senegal_gender_security.pdf (Accessed December 17, 2012).

Reilly, Niamh. 2009. *Women's Human Rights.* Cambridge, UK: Polity Press.

Reingold, Beth. 2008. "Women as Office Holders: Linking Descriptive and Substantive
Representation." In Christina Wolbrecht, Karen Beckwith, and Lisa Baldez, eds.,
Political Women and American Democracy. New York: Cambridge University Press.

Remenyi, Maria. 2007. "The Multiple Faces of the Intersections between HIV and Violence against Women: Development Connections." Washington, DC: Development
Connections, UNIFEM, Pan American Health Organization, Inter-American Commission for Women, and the Latin American and Caribbean Women's Health Network.

Renzetti, Claire. 2011. "Economic Issues and Intimate Partner Violence." In Claire M.
Renzetti, Jeffrey L. Edleson, Raquel Kennedy Bergen, eds., *Sourcebook on Violence
against Women.* Washington, DC: Sage.

Reynolds, Andrew. 1999. "Women in the Legislatures and Executives of the World:
Knocking at the Highest Glass Ceiling." *World Politics* 51(4): 547

Reynolds, Thomas H., and Arturo A. Flores. 2012. *Foreign Law Guide: Current Sources
of Codes and Basic Legislation in Jurisdictions of the World.* Boston: Martinus Nijhoff
Publishers. http://www.foreignlawguide.com (Accessed December 17, 2012).

Richards, David and Ronald Gelleny. 2007. "Women's Status and Economic Globalization." *International Studies Quarterly* 51(4): 855–876.

Richards, David, and Jillienne Haglund. 2013. Violence against Women Dataset.

Rigaux, François. 1998. "Hans Kelsen on International Law." *European Journal of
International Law* 9: 325–343.

Riggs, David S., Marie B. Caulfield, and Amy E. Street. 2000. "Risk for Domestic Violence: Factors Associated with Perpetration and Victimization." *Journal of Clinical
Psychology* 56(10): 1289–1316.

Rihani, May. 2006. "Keeping the Promise: Five Benefits of Girls' Secondary Education."
Academy for Educational Development. http://www.ungei.org/resources/files
/aed_keepingpromise.pdf (Accessed December 17, 2013).

Risse, Thomas, and Kathryn Sikkink. 1999. "The Socialization of International Human
Rights Norms Into Domestic Practices: Introduction." In Thomas Risse, Stephen C.
Ropp, and Kathryn Sikkink, eds., *The Power of Human Rights: International Norms
and Domestic Change.* New York: Cambridge University Press.

Rodrik, Dani. 1998. "Has Globalization Gone Too Far?" *Challenge* 4(1):81–94.

Rogowski, Ronald. 1987. "Political Cleavages and Changing Exposure to Trade." *American Political Science Review* 81(4): 1121–1137.

Romany, Celia. 1994. "State Responsibility Goes Private: A Feminist Critique of the
Public/Private Distinction in Human Rights Law." In Rebecca Cook, ed., *Human
Rights of Women.* Philadelphia: University of Pennsylvania Press.

Ross, Susan Deller. 2008. *Women's Human Rights: The International and Comparative Law Casebook.* Philadelphia: University of Pennsylvania Press.

Rubalcava, Luis, Graciela Teruel, and Duncan Thomas. 2009. "Investments, Time Preferences, and Public Transfers Paid to Women." *Economic Development and Cultural Change* 57(3): 507–538.

Russell, Diana E. H. 1975. *The Politics of Rape.* New York, NY: Stein and Day.

Sabatier, Paul A., and Hank C. Jenkins-Smith. 1999. *Theories of the Policy Process.* Boulder, CO: Westview Press.

Saguy, Abigail C. 2003. *What Is Sexual Harassment? From Capitol Hill to the Sorbonne.* Berkeley: University of California Press.

Saint-Germain, Michelle. 1989. "Does Their Difference Make a Difference? The Impact of Women on Public Policy in the Arizona Legislature." *Social Science Quarterly* 70(4): 956–68.

Saletan, William. 2012. "Mourdock Isn't on GOP Fringe." *Philadelphia Inquirer.* October 29. http://www.philly.com/philly/opinion/inquirer/20121029_Mourdock _isn_t_on_GOP_fringe.html (Accessed October 29, 2012).

Saltzman, Linda E., Janet L. Fanslow, Pamela M. McMahon, and Gene A. Shelley. 1999. *Intimate Partner Violence Surveillance: Uniform Definitions and Recommended Data Elements, version 1.0.* Atlanta: Centers for Disease Control and Prevention, National Center for Injury Prevention and Control. http://www.cdc.gov/ncipc/pub-res/ipv _surveillance/Intimate%20Partner%20Violence.pdf (Accessed March 1, 2013).

Salzman, Todd A. 2006. "Rape Camps as a Means of Ethnic Cleansing: Religious, Cultural, and Ethical Responses to Rape Victims in the Former Yugoslavia." In Bert B. Lockwood, ed., *Women's Rights: A Human Rights Quarterly Reader.* Baltimore: The Johns Hopkins University Press.

Santos, Cecilia MacDowell. 2005. *Women's Police Stations: Gender, Violence, and Justice in São Paulo, Brazil.* New York: Palgrave Macmillan.

Sarfaty, Galit A. 2009. "Why Culture Matters in International Institutions: The Marginality of Human Rights at the World Bank." *American Journal of International Law* 103: 647–683.

Scanzoni, John, and Cynthia Arnett. 1987. "Enlarging the Understanding of Marital Commitment via Religious Devoutness, Gender Role Preferences, and Locus of Marital Control." *Journal of Family Issues* 8(1): 136–156.

Schedler, Andreas. 2012. "The Measurer's Dilemma: Coordination Failures in Cross-National Political Data Collection." *Comparative Political Studies* 45(2): 237–266.

Schlafly, Roger. 2012. "What VAWA Is About." *Eagle Forum Blog.* May 18. http://blog .eagleforum.org/2012/05/what-vawa-is-about.html (Accessed October 26, 2012).

Schneider, Elizabeth, Cheryl Hanna, Judith G. Greenberg, and Clare Dalton. 2008. *Domestic Violence and the Law: Theory and Practice.* New York: Foundation Press.

Schrodt, Philip A. 2006. "Beyond the Linear Frequentist Orthodoxy." *Political Analysis* 14(3): 335–339.

Schuler, Margaret, ed. 1992. *Freedom from Violence: Women's Strategies from Around the World*. New York: UNIFEM.

Sen, Amartya. 2003. "Missing Women—Revisited." *British Medical Journal* 327(7427): 1297–1298.

Sharabi, Hisham. 1988. *Neopatriarchy: A Theory of Distorted Change in Arab Society*. New York: Oxford University Press.

Shepard, Melanie, and Ellen Pence. 1988. "The Effects of Battering on the Employment Status of Women." *Affilia* 3(2): 55–61.

Simmons, Beth A. 2009. *Mobilizing for Human Rights: International Law in Domestic Politics*. New York: Cambridge University Press.

Simmons, Beth A., and Daniel J. Hopkins. 2005. "The Constraining Power of International Treaties: Theory and Methods." *American Political Science Review* 99(4): 623–631.

Slaughter, Anne-Marie. 1995. "International Law in a World of Liberal States." *European Journal of International Law* 6(1): 503–538.

Sommers, Marilyn Sawyer. 2007. "Defining Patterns of Genital Injury from Sexual Assault: A Review." *Trauma, Violence, and Abuse* 8(3):270–280.

Soto, Lucy. 1992. "Marital Rape Acquittal Fuels Debate." Associated Press. April 18. http://news.google.com/newspapers?nid=1346&dat=19920418&id=ToYwAAA AIBAJ&sjid=PfwDAAAAIBAJ&pg=6810,4798455 (Accessed August 5, 2013).

Spees, Pam. 2003. "Women's Advocacy in the Creation of the International Criminal Court: Changing the Landscapes of Justice and Power." *Journal of Women in Culture and Society* 28(4): 1233–1254.

Spirer, Herbert F. 1990. "Violations of Human Rights. How Many? The Statistical Problems of Measuring Such Infractions Are Tough, but Statistical Science Is Equal to It." *American Journal of Economics and Sociology* 49(2): 199–210.

Spivak, Gayatri Chakravorty. 1988. "Subaltern Studies: Deconstructing Historiography." In Ranajit Guha and Gayatri Chakravorty Spivak, eds., *Selected Subaltern Studies*. New York: Oxford University Press.

Spohn, Cassia, and Julie Horney. 1992. *Rape Law Reform: A Grassroots Revolution and Its Impact*. New York: Springer.

Stack, Sarah. 2011. "Recession Blamed for Massive Increase in Domestic Violence." *Irish Independent*. August 29. http://www.independent.ie/irish-news/recession-blamed -for-massive-increase-in-domestic-violence-26765996.html (Accessed December 17, 2013).

Stark, Evan, and Anne H. Flitcraft. 1991. "Spouse Abuse." In Mark L. Rosenberg and Marty Ann Fenley, eds., *Violence in America: A Public Health Approach*. New York: Oxford University Press.

Street, Amy E., Jane Stafford, Clare M. Mahan, and Ann Hendricks. 2008. "Sexual

Harassment and Assault Experienced by Reservists during Military Service." *Journal of Rehabilitation Research and Development* 45(3): 409–420.

Sylvester, Christine. 1994. *Feminist Theory and International Relations in a Postmodern Era*. New York: Cambridge University Press.

Tashman, Brian. 2012. "Violence against Women Act: Roger Schlafly Denounces Violence against Women Act, Dismisses Congresswoman Who Sought Charges against Her Rapist." People for the American Way, Right Wing Watch. May 19. http://www.rightwingwatch.org/content/roger-schlafly-denounces-violence-against-women-act-dismisses-congresswoman-who-sought-charg (Accessed October 29, 2012).

Thomas, Dorothy and Michele Beaseley. 1993. "Domestic Violence as a Human Rights Issue." *Human Rights Quarterly* 15(1): 36–62.

Thomas, Duncan. 1990. "Intra-Household Resource Allocation: An Inferential Approach." *Journal of Human Resources* 25(4): 635–664.

———. 1992. "The Distribution of Income and Expenditures within the Household." *Annales d'Economie et de Statistique* 29(1): 109–136.

Thomas, Sue. 1991. "The Impact of Women on State Legislative Policies." *Journal of Politics* 53(4): 958–976.

———. 1994. *How Women Legislate*. New York: Oxford University Press.

Tickner, J. Ann. 2006. "Feminism Meets International Relations: Some Methodological Issues." In Brooke A. Ackerly, Maria Stern, and Jacqui True, eds., *Feminist Methodologies for International Relations*. New York: Cambridge University Press.

Tindigarukayo, Jimmy. 2006. "Perceptions and Reflections on Sexual Harassment in Jamaica." *Journal of International Women's Studies* 7(4): 90–110.

Tjaden, Patricia, and Nancy Thoennes. 1998. *Prevalence, Incidence, and Consequences of Violence against Women: Findings from the National Violence against Women Survey*. Washington, DC: National Institute of Justice. https://www.ncjrs.gov/pdffiles/172837.pdf (Accessed December 17, 2013).

———. 2000. *Extent, Nature, and Consequences of Intimate Partner Violence: Findings From the National Violence against Women Survey*. NCJ 181867. Washington, DC: US Department of Justice, Office of Justice Programs.

———. 2006. *Extent, Nature, and Consequences of Rape Victimization: Findings from the National Violence against Women Survey*. NCJ 210346. Washington, DC: US Department of Justice, Office of Justice Programs.

Tòth, Zsófia. 2010. "Domestic Violence—Legal Background and Support System in Hungary." Presented at the European Seminar on Domestic Violence, November 24–26, Paris. http://www.cepprobation.org/uploaded_files/Pres%20STARR%20Par%20Toth.pdf (Accessed December 20, 2012).

Tremblay, Manon. 1998. "Do Female MPs Substantively Represent Women? A Study of Legislative Behavior in Canada's 35th Parliament." *Canadian Journal of Political Science* 31(3): 435–65.

True, Jacqui. 2012. *The Political Economy of Violence against Women*. New York: Oxford University Press.

Tsanga, Amy S. 2007. "Reconceptualizing the Role of Legal Information Dissemination in the Context of Legal Pluralism in African Settings." In Anne Hellum, Julie Stewart, Shaheen Sardar Ali, and Amy Tsanga, eds., *Human Rights, Plural Legalities, and Gendered Realities: Paths Are Made by Walking*. Harare, Zimbabwe: Weaver Press.

Ulrich, Jennifer L. 2000. "Confronting Gender-Based Violence with International Instruments: Is a Solution to the Pandemic within Reach?" *Journal of Global Legal Studies* 7(2): 629–654.

United Nations. 1948. Universal Declaration of Human Rights (UDHR). http://www .ohchr.org/EN/UDHR/Documents/UDHR_Translations/eng.pdf (Accessed November 9, 2012).

———. 1966a. International Covenant on Civil and Political Rights. http://www2 .ohchr.org/english/law/ccpr.htm (Accessed November 9, 2012).

———. 1966b. International Covenant on Economic, Social, and Cultural Rights. http:// www2.ohchr.org/english/law/cescr.htm (Accessed November 9, 2012).

———. 1969. Vienna Convention on the Laws of Treaties. http://untreaty.un.org/ilc/texts /instruments/english/conventions/1_1_1969.pdf (Accessed November 9, 2012).

———. 1979. Convention on the Elimination of All Forms of Violence against Women. http://www.un.org/womenwatch/daw/cedaw/text/econvention.htm (Accessed November 9, 2012).

———. 1992. "General Recommendation No. 19: Violence against Women." 11th Session. http://www.un.org/womenwatch/daw/cedaw/recommendations/recomm .htm (Accessed November 9, 2012).

———. 1993. Vienna Declaration and Programme of Action. Doc. A/CONF.157/23, 12 July 1993. http://www.ohchr.org/en/professionalinterest/pages/vienna.aspx (Accessed September 16, 2014).

———. 1996. Report on the Situation of Human Rights in Rwanda. United Nations Special Rapporteur on the Situation of Human Rights in Rwanda E/CN/1996/68.

———. 2004. *Teaching Human Rights: Practical Activities for Primary and Secondary Schools*. Geneva, Switzerland: United Nations High Commissioner for Human Rights.

———. 2012. "Reservations to CEDAW." http://www.un.org/womenwatch/daw /cedaw/reservations.htm (Accessed November 9, 2012).

United Nations Children's Fund (UNICEF). 2010. "Legislative Reform to Support the Abandonment of Female Genital Mutilation/Cutting." http://www.unicef.org /policyanalysis/files/UNICEF_-_LRI_Legislative_Reform_to_support_the _Abandonment_of_FGMC_August_2010.pdf (Accessed January 10, 2013).

United Nations Declaration on the Elimination of Violence against Women (DEVAW). 1993. GA res. A/RES/48/104, 20 December 1993. http://www.un.org /documents/ga/res/48/a48r104.htm (Accessed December 17, 2013).

United Nations Division for the Advancement of Women (UNDAW). 2007. "Indicators to Measure Violence against Women" Expert Group Meeting. http://www.un.org/womenwatch/daw/egm/IndicatorsVAW/IndicatorsVAW_EGM_report.pdf (Accessed December 17, 2012).

———. 2009. The UN Secretary-General's Database on Violence against Women. http://webapps01.un.org/vawdatabase/home.action (Accessed August 3, 2009).

———. 2010. *Handbook for Legislation on Violence against Women*. ST/ESA/329. http://www.un.org/womenwatch/daw//vaw/handbook/Handbook%20for%20legislation%20on%20violence%20against%20women.pdf (Accessed August 5, 2013).

———. 2013. Section 357 of the Criminal Code and Section 282 of the Penal Code. The UN Secretary-General's Database on Violence against Women. http://sgdatabase.unwomen.org/searchDetail.action?measureId=10511&baseHREF=country&baseHREFId=976 (Accessed August 5, 2013).

United Nations Entity for Gender Equality and the Empowerment of Women (UN Women). 2008. "Prohibition of Discrimination, Harassment, Including Sexual Harassment, and Abuse of Authority." http://www.un.org/womenwatch/osagi/fpsexualharassment.htm (Accessed January 24, 2013).

———. 2012. *2011–2012 Progress of the World's Women: In Pursuit of Justice*. http://progress.unwomen.org/pdfs/EN-Report-Progress.pdf (Accessed December 17, 2012).

United Nations General Assembly. 2011. "Strengthening Crime Prevention and Criminal Justice Responses to Violence against Women." Resolution 65/228. http://www.unodc.org/documents/justice-and-prison-reform/crimeprevention/Model_Strategies_and_Practical_Measures_on_the_Elimination_of_Violence_against_Women_in_the_Field_of_Crime_Prevention_and_Criminal_Justice.pdf (Accessed August 13, 2013).

United Nations Population Fund (UNFPA). 2000. *The State of World Population 2000: Ending Violence against Women and Girls, A Human Rights and Health Priority*. New York: UNFPA.

———. 2008. *The State of the World Population 2008: Culture, Gender, and Human Rights*. New York: UNFPA.

United Nations Research Institute for Social Development (UNRISD). 2005. "Gender Equality: Striving for Justice in an Unequal World." http://www.unrisd.org/80256B3C005BCCF9/search/1FF4AC64C1894EAAC1256FA3005E7201?OpenDocument (Accessed August 18, 2014).

United Nations Security Council (UNSC). 2002. Report of the Secretary General on Women, Peace, and Security. http://www.securitycouncilreport.org/atf/cf/%7B65BFCF9B-6D27-4E9C-8CD3-CF6E4FF96FF9%7D/s_2012_732.pdf (Accessed January 25, 2013).

———. 2008. Resolution 1820. http://www.state.gov/documents/organization/106577.pdf (Accessed January 25, 2013).

United Nations Treaty Collection Database. 2013. Convention on the Elimination of All Forms of Discrimination against Women—Status. https://treaties.un.org/Pages/ViewDetails.aspx?src=TREATY&mtdsg_no=IV-8&chapter=4&lang=en (Accessed January 3, 2013).

US Department of State. Annual. Country Reports on Human Rights Practices. http://www.state.gov/j/drl/rls/hrrpt/ (Accessed December 19, 2012).

———. 2008a. "Nigeria." 2007 Country Reports on Human Rights Practices. http://www.state.gov/j/drl/rls/hrrpt/2007/100498.htm (Accessed August 5, 2013).

———. 2008b. "Saint Lucia." 2007 Country Reports on Human Rights Practices. http://www.state.gov/j/drl/rls/hrrpt/2008/wha/119172.htm (Accessed August 5, 2013).

———. 2008c. "Burundi." 2007 Country Reports on Human Rights Practices. http://www.state.gov/j/drl/rls/hrrpt/2008/af/118989.htm (Accessed August 5, 2013).

———. 2009a. "Argentina." 2008 Country Reports on Human Rights Practices. http://www.state.gov/j/drl/rls/hrrpt/2008/wha/119145.htm (Accessed August 5, 2013).

———. 2009b. "Nigeria." 2008 Country Reports on Human Rights Practices. http://www.state.gov/j/drl/rls/hrrpt/2008/wha/119172.htm (Accessed August 5, 2013).

———. 2009c. "Saint Lucia." 2008 Country Reports on Human Rights Practices. http://www.state.gov/j/drl/rls/hrrpt/2009/wha/136125.htm (Accessed August 5, 2013).

———. 2009d. "Morocco." 2008 Country Reports on Human Rights Practices. http://www.state.gov/j/drl/rls/hrrpt/2009/nea/136075.htm (Accessed August 5, 2013).

———. 2009e. "Senegal." 2008 Country Reports on Human Rights Practices. http://www.state.gov/j/drl/rls/hrrpt/2008/af/119021.htm (Accessed December 17, 2012).

———. 2010a. "Nigeria." 2009 Country Reports on Human Rights Practices. http://www.state.gov/j/drl/rls/hrrpt/2010/af/154363.htm (Accessed August 5, 2013).

———. 2010b. "Iraq." 2010 Country Reports on Human Rights Practices. http://www.state.gov/j/drl/rls/hrrpt/2010/nea/154462.htm (Accessed January 10, 2014).

———. 2011. "Nigeria." 2010 Country Reports on Human Rights Practices. http://www.state.gov/j/drl/rls/hrrpt/humanrightsreport/index.htm?dlid=186229 (Accessed August 5, 2013).

United States Merit Systems Protection Board. 1994. "Sexual Harassment in the Federal Workplace: Trends, Progress and Continuing Challenges." http://www.mspb.gov/netsearch/viewdocs.aspx?docnumber=253661&version=253948&application=ACROBAT (Accessed January 24, 2013).

University of Pretoria Centre for Human Rights. 2011. "Submission to the Universal Periodic Review of Swaziland." March 14. http://lib.ohchr.org/HRBodies/UPR/Documents/session12/SZ/CHR-CentreHumanRightsUniversityPretoria-eng.pdf (Accessed August 5, 2013).

van Woudenberg, Anneke. 2012. "Confronting Rape as a Weapon of War in the Democratic Republic of Congo. The Impact of Armed Conflict on Women and Girls."

In Minky Worden, ed., *The Unfinished Revolution: Voices from the Global Fight for Women's Rights*. New York: Seven Stories Press, 129–138.

van Gulik, Gauri. 2012. "Behind Closed Doors: Domestic Violence in Europe." In Minky Worden, ed., *The Unfinished Revolution: Voices from the Global Fight for Women's Rights*. New York: Seven Stories Press, 221–230.

Vega, Arturo, and Juanita M. Firestone. 1995. "The Effects of Gender on Congressional Behavior and the Substantive Representation of Women." *Legislative Studies Quarterly* 20(2): 213–222.

Vijayalakshmi V. 2002. "Gender, Accountability, and Political Representation in Local Government." Working Paper No. 102, The Institute for Social and Economic Change, Bangalore. http://203.200.22.249:8080/jspui/bitstream/123456789/1904/1/Gender_accountability_and_political.pdf (Accessed December 17, 2013).

von Bernstorff, Jochen. 2008. "The Changing Fortunes of the Universal Declaration of Human Rights: Genesis and Symbolic Dimensions of the Turn to Rights in International Law." *European Journal of International Law* 19(5): 903–924.

Walter, Barbara F. 1997. "The Critical Barrier to Civil War Settlement." *International Organization* 51(3): 335–364.

Ward, Jeanne. 2002. *If Not Now, When? Addressing Gender-Based Violence in Refugee, Internally Displaced, and Post-Conflict Settings, A Global Overview*. New York: The Reproductive Health for Refugees Consortium. http://www.rhrc.org/resources/gbv/ifnotnow.html (Accessed August 18, 2014).

Ward, Jeanne and Mendy Marsh. 2006. "Sexual Violence against Women and Girls in War and Its Aftermath: Realities, Responses, and Required Resources: A Briefing Paper." Brussels, Belgium: United Nations Population Fund. http://www.unfpa.org/emergencies/symposium06/docs/finalbrusselsbriefingpaper.pdf (Accessed January 25, 2013).

Watts, Charlotte, and Cathy Zimmerman. 2002. "Violence against Women: Global Scope and Magnitude." *Lancet* 359(9313): 1232–1237.

Webb, Susan. 1994. *Shockwaves: The Global Impact of Sexual Harassment*. New York: Mastermedia Publishing Company.

Welch, Susan, and Sue Thomas. 1991. "Do Women in Public Office Make a Difference?" In Debra L. Dodson, ed., *Gender and Policymaking: Studies of Women in Office*. The Impact of Women in Public Office Project. Rutgers, NJ: Center for the American Woman and Politics.

Weidmann, Nils B., Doreen Kuse, and Kristian Skrede Gleditsch. 2010. "The Geography of the International System: The CShapes Dataset. *International Interactions* 36(1): 86–106.

Weldon, S. Laurel. 2002. *Protest, Policy, and the Problem of Violence against Women*. Pittsburgh: University of Pittsburgh Press.

———. 2006. "Inclusion and Understanding: A Collective Methodology for Feminist

International Relations." In Brooke A. Ackerly, Maria Stern, and Jacqui True, eds., *Feminist Methodologies for International Relations*. New York: Cambridge University Press.

Whatley, M. A. 1993. "For Better or Worse: The Case of Marital Rape." *Violence and Victims* 8(1): 29–39.

Williams, Jody. 2012. "Devastating Remnants of War: The Impact of Armed Conflict on Women and Girls." In Minky Worden, ed., *The Unfinished Revolution: Voices from the Global Fight for Women's Rights*. New York: Seven Stories Press, 109–116.

Willness, Chelea R., Piers Steel, and Kibeom Lee. 2007. "A Meta-Analysis of Antecedents of Workplace Sexual Harassment." *Personnel Psychology* 60(1): 127–162.

Wilson, Amanda. 2011. "Rights Commission Rebukes U.S. on Domestic Violence." *Inter Press Service News Agency*. August 19. http://www.ipsnews.net/2011/08/rights -commission-rebukes-us-on-domestic-violence/ (Accessed December 17, 2013).

Wise, Sue, and Liz Stanely. 1987. *Georgie Porgie: Sexual Harassment in Everyday Life*. London: Pandora Press.

World Bank. 2001. "Engendering Development: Through Gender Equality in Rights, Resources, and Voice." World Bank Policy Research Report No. 21776.

———. 2004. *Gender and Development in the Middle East and North Africa*. Washington, DC: World Bank.

———. 2013. World Development Indicators. http://data.worldbank.org/indicator (Accessed January 3, 2013).

World Health Organization (WHO). 1997a. "Violence against Women in Situations of Armed Conflict and Displacement." http://www.who.int/gender/violence/v7.pdf (Accessed January 25, 2013).

———. 1997b. "Violence against Women: Health Consequences." http://www.who .int/gender/violence/v8.pdf (Accessed February 1, 2013).

———. 2000. *Female Genital Mutilation: A Handbook for Frontline Workers*. Geneva: World Health Organization. http://whqlibdoc.who.int/hq/2000/WHO_FCH _WMH_00.5_eng.pdf (Accessed December 17, 2013).

———. 2005. *WHO Multi-country Study on Women's Health and Domestic Violence against Women: Initial Results on Prevalence, Health Outcomes, and Women's Responses*. Geneva: World Health Organization. http://www.who.int/gender /violence/who_multicountry_study/summary_report/summary_report_English2 .pdf?ua=1 (Accessed June 23, 2014).

———. 2006. *A Factual Overview of Female Genital Mutilation. Progress in Sexual and Reproductive Health*. No. 72. Geneva: World Health Organization. http://www .who.int/reproductivehealth/topics/fgm/progress72_fgm.pdf (Accessed December 17, 2013).

Woudenberg, Anneke Van. 2012. "Confronting Rape as a Weapon of War in the Democratic Republic of Congo. The Impact of Armed Conflict on Women and Girls."

In *The Unfinished Revolution: Voices from the Global Fight for Women's Rights,* ed. Minky Worden. New York: Seven Stories Press, 129–138.

Young, Iris Marion. 1997. *Intersecting Voices: Dilemmas of Gender, Political Philosophy, and Policy.* Princeton, NJ: Princeton University Press.

———. 2000. *Inclusion and Democracy.* Oxford: Oxford University Press.

Zierler, Sally, William Cunningham, Ron Andersen, Martin Shapiro, Sam A. Bozzette, Terry Nakazono, Sally Morton, Stephen Crystal, Michael Stein, Barbara Turner, and Patti St. Clair. 2000. "Violence Victimization after HIV Infection in a US Probability Sample of Adult Patients in Primary Care." *American Journal of Public Health* 90(3): 208–215.

INDEX

ABOUT THE AUTHORS

David L. Richards is associate professor of political science and human rights at the University of Connecticut. He was the cofounder and codirector of the CIRI Human Rights Data Project and has published wide-ranging research on human rights in numerous professional journals and books. He lives in the Quiet Corner of Connecticut with his wife and children.

Jillienne Haglund is a postdoctoral research associate in political science at Washington University in Saint Louis, Missouri, and will join the political science department at the University of Kentucky as an assistant professor in the Fall 2015. She earned a PhD in political science at Florida State University in August 2014, a master of arts in political science at the University of Memphis in 2009, and bachelor of arts in political science at Montana State University–Bozeman in 2007.